I Don't Wish Nobody to
Have a Life Like Mine

I Don't Wish Nobody to Have a Life Like Mine

Tales of Kids in Adult Lockup

David Chura

Beacon Press, Boston

Beacon Press
25 Beacon Street
Boston, Massachusetts 02108–2892
www.beacon.org

Beacon Press books
are published under the auspices of
the Unitarian Universalist Association of Congregations.

13   12   11   10   8   7   6   5   4   3   2   1

This book is printed on acid-free paper that meets the uncoated paper
ANSI/NISO specifications for permanence as revised in 1992.

Text design by Yvonne Tsang
at Wilsted & Taylor Publishing Services

Library of Congress Cataloging-in-Publication Data

Chura, David.
I don't wish nobody to have a life like mine :
tales of kids in adult lockup / David Chura.
p. cm.
ISBN 978-0-8070-0064-9 (hbk. : alk. paper) 1. Chura, David, 1948– 2. Juvenile
delinquents—Education—New York (State) 3. Prisoners—Education—New York
(State) 4. Prisons—New York (State) 5. Corrections—New York (State) I. Title.
HV9105.N7C456 2010
371.93092—dc22
[B]   2009027664

"Prison Birthday: It's All Good" appeared in *Contemporary Justice Review* 5, No. 1
(February 2002). Published by Taylor & Francis Group. Reprinted by permission of
the publisher (Taylor & Francis Group, www.informaworld.com). "Pin-Ups"
appeared in *Fourth Genre: Explorations in Nonfiction* 7, No. 1 (Spring 2005).
Published by Michigan State University Press.

For Rick

Contents

Introduction

In 1995, I started teaching high school kids locked up in a New York county jail after working with at-risk teens for thirteen years in a community alternative school. Somehow I always knew I'd end up in jail. Maybe it was the company I'd kept over the years. Inner city kids, homeless old guys, and soup kitchen moms lined up to feed their children, teenagers pushed to the margins of society by drugs and by families and communities that didn't want them.

My eyes were opened during the '60s to the "other America," the poor, the disenfranchised, the outsider. I got my first lessons in the millstone life of poverty and neglect the summer before college when I worked at an inner city neighborhood center in upstate New York where I grew up. Then, while I was in college, I helped out at a homeless shelter serving meals, giving out clothes, and listening to the desperate stories of the people whose lives and worlds had crumbled around them.

But the people who came to the shelter weren't the only ones being pushed to the edge of society by a country at war with itself. Young men my age were being drafted to fight in Vietnam. Many fought, many refused, many died, and my friends and I stood at the gravesites of more than one classmate. Until I came to my own decision. I dropped out of college to file for conscientious objector status and, for my alternative service, worked in a psychiatric hospital in Westchester County, an affluent suburb of metropolitan New York, with young people abandoned by families, friends, and in many case, reason itself.

When I returned to college to complete my degree in literature and in psychology—combining my two passions—I knew that I wanted to work with troubled teens because by then I saw that they were the real casualties of our culture, society's young throwaways, fundamentally homeless whether living on the streets, in derelict cars, or in overcrowded shelters; in poorly funded and poorly run group homes; or in families, intact or splintered, ravished by drugs and alcohol, crime and violence, abuse and neglect, poverty and disease.

For several years after college, I worked in a community crisis center training other counselors and helping clients, mostly young people, through the dilemmas that crippled their lives and happiness. Then, after several years of doing this intense intervention work, I decided the classroom would be the place where I could engage kids in the more positive aspects of who they were—their energy, their creativity, their fresh way of looking at the world—and give them a reprieve from the chorus of woe that sirened through their lives.

In 1982, I walked into my first classroom as an English teacher at a regional alternative high school in Westchester. The program was designed to work with kids from across the county whose districts couldn't handle them. Although students were expected to follow the same standardized curriculum as their counterparts in their previous schools, how that was done was left up to the resourcefulness and tenacity of the teaching staff.

In the 1980s and the early '90s, many districts used alternative education as dumping grounds. The young people sent to these programs were seen as trouble—to teachers and administrators, to the neighborhood, to the police, to the community. They were rarely seen as what they really were—trouble to themselves: the senior graduating as a result of social promotion who still couldn't read past a third-grade level; the bright but pregnant fifteen-year-old who was college-bound, but now couldn't get herself up in the morning and on the bus; the drug user and the drug dealer who were more addicted to the streets than to school; the kid who couldn't let a rule go by without challenging it and the teacher who issued it; the special ed student whose classification was dropped to save a district money; the fighter, the isolate, the bully, the victim.

Yet, while the districts might have seen alternative schools as dumping grounds, the students and staff in these programs saw them as safe havens. My school was small, personal, and tolerant. Even though students came from a variety of towns—rich and poor, rural and suburban, diverse and segregated by money or race— everyone, including the principal, was on a first-name basis. It was a small attempt to bring down "the system" that had tripped up so many of our kids with its rules and regulations.

For most of my years at the school, there was a calm and security that many of my public schoolteacher friends reported was rapidly eroding in their classrooms with stories of guns, gangs, and teacher assaults. Our students might have been trouble elsewhere, they might have resented being kicked out of their home districts and banished from their towns for eight hours a day, but for them the alternative school was a refuge, and they kept it that way.

Then in the early '90s things began to change. Schools were pressured for more student accountability. More standardized tests were introduced; course requirements were increased; and attendance and dropout rates were more closely looked at, at the same time that education budgets were getting tighter.

As a result, students who before might have been subtly encouraged to drop out; shunted off to GED programs; or put on homebound tutoring (a sure bet, in my experience, that a student would disappear—a quick solution to the district's attendance problem), as well as those with addiction or emotional problems, were shipped out to alternative programs like ours. Now, the kids getting off the school buses from their hometowns were angrier, more troubled, more reckless, more hounded by the wolves—crack, AIDS, guns, abuse—that increasingly hunted the hood.

At the same time, the media was increasingly filled with stories about out of control teenagers. We were told that America was a riot of carjackings; gang wars; random and senseless violence; attacks against ordinary middle-class citizens. Although teenage crime—grist for the local news mill—has always been overreported (even though it accounts for only 40 percent of violent crime statistics overall), the national media more and more sensationalized and, in a perverse way, romanticized it.

The war on crime was brewing into a war on kids.

But as those of us who worked with the young people demonized by this coverage knew, only one side of the story was being told. News reports rarely told about families shattered by crushing economic pressures and unemployment; decaying neighborhoods; or about grandmothers burdened with second families birthed by the loss of an adult child—and parent—to addiction or disease. And rarely reported were the desperate lives these teens led in juvenile care, rehabs, or psych hospitals, or—when all else failed—on the open road.

Yet, in the face of all this, the alternative school where I taught remained a sanctuary even while, like everywhere else around us, our budget and staff were cut despite our population's neediness. Some days it was more like a triage center and emergency room than a school; but we all worked to maintain that sense of security.

Until one day the campus erupted, the police were called, and safety disappeared.

Bono was one of those new, more damaged kids. At fourteen, the smallest and youngest boy on campus, everybody liked him, so everybody liked picking on him in that good-natured "talking trash" way that adolescents get into. But good-natured "talking trash" became trash, and Bono had had enough. Before the staff knew what was happening, kids poured out of the classrooms into the parking lot ready to settle scores none of us knew they were keeping, swinging fists and knives and weights stolen from the gym. In the confusion of attack and arbitration, I was knocked down. After the police were called and the melee was over, and I found my glasses, I began to see things differently.

As hard as everyone had tried to keep the streets at bay, our school had become just as risky, as vulnerable as the neighborhoods my students came from. The trust we had fostered was broken. We—national and state policy makers, school districts, administrators, teachers, and students—had failed and betrayed each other. After that day the kids ignored their own long-held tenet against the world—"don't believe the hype!"—and set out to prove that the news industry, the school districts, and the communities that had rejected them were right: they were as bad as everybody said they were.

After thirteen years at the alternative school, frustrated by the budgetary constraints that made it impossible to adequately deal with the changes in our student population, I decided in 1995 to transfer to another alternative high school. The Incarcerated Youth Program taught high-school-aged men and women locked up in the Westchester County jail, an adult facility which housed up to eighteen hundred inmates.

New York state education law mandates that any school-age inmate be provided with the same education he or she would receive in their home schools. So unlike in community schools, where districts could drop students from a program, or pull them back into the regular high school in order to save money, the jailhouse school was secure. Fortunately—and unfortunately—our enrollment, stable at about 120, was never threatened: kids got in trouble, police arrested them, and the districts paid for their education.

I had no illusions about what I was walking into. I knew that the young people I'd meet in prison would be a distillation of the toughest ones I had worked with at the community alternative. They wouldn't be at-risk because by then they would've already fallen in harm's way, already fallen "over the edge" that so many of my community students had teetered on, fallen into the world of adult jail—a world of violence, squalor, and isolation that no child should ever have to face, let alone live in for months or years.

Despite their young age—some barely fifteen—the jail students had long ago exhausted juvenile care and detention. For years, many had been in and out of family court, at first there for their parents' neglect and abuse, then for their own misdemeanors. In many cases they had been taken from what tattered remnants of family they had and placed in foster care.

Since the only stability these youngsters knew was as a part of the child welfare system (an unwanted part at that), foster care often led to group homes, to residential centers, to juvenile detention, or to rehab, a cycle that played itself out through their early years. Some even ended up being farmed out to programs in other states when all other options had been exhausted. For many, these out-of-state placements, that exiled them hundreds of miles away from family and friends, were harshest of all. One young inmate who had never been outside of Yonkers (New York's fourth largest city) and who had been in a lot of tough placements, talked about his year in a Berkshire Mountain facility as the worst year of his life. "It was nothing but woods and snow—and who knows what kinda wild animals were out there," he told me, shuddering.

Life for these locked up kids had been a spiral of neglect that led nowhere but down, until they crash-dived into places like New York City's notorious Spofford, or Woodfield Cottage, a secure juvenile facility that a *New York Times* reporter described as "Westchester's equivalent of a Rikers Island for juvenile offenders."

But they hadn't stopped there. Many had already been in and out of the real Rikers Island and various other county jails; some had even done time in different state prisons.

Somehow, knowing what I'd be dealing with, and knowing that everyone else involved—the supervisors, the other teachers, the correctional staff, even the inmates themselves—would also know, the job, while certainly challenging, seemed doable and potentially rewarding.

Then, during my first year at the jail, a new battle cry in the crime war was sounded.

John Dilulio, a political scientist and social commentator, wrote an article in 1995 for the Philadelphia *Weekly Standard* entitled "The Coming of the Super-predators." Using district attorneys, law enforcement officials, and even adult inmates as his sources, Dilulio stated that the kids committing crimes in a "youth crime wave [that] has reached horrific proportions from coast to coast" are some of the worse this country has seen. Whatever his intent, his language was incendiary. He described these young people as "hardened remorseless juveniles" who are "totally out of control" with "no respect for human life... capable of committing the most heinous acts of physical violence for the most trivial reasons."

But that wasn't the worst of it.

He went on to warn that "Americans were sitting atop a demographic crime bomb" that "will unleash an army of young predatory male street criminals." For him the math was simple: forty million children under the age of ten—the largest number in decades—would soon become a startling and alarming number of fourteen- to seventeen-year-olds. In ten years, "the number of males in this age group will have risen about 25 percent overall and 50 percent for blacks."

Although many academics and social commentators quickly disputed Dilulio's predictions and analysis (one criminologist criticized his forecasts as "hyperbolic proclamations," while a law professor pointed out that many of Dilulio's "super-predators" "have yet to be born") his ideas even more quickly made it into the mass media. They captured the frightened, yet at the same time, fascinated imagination of the public as "juvenile delinquents" escalated into "super-predators"—and they were everywhere.

Newspapers across the country reported these provocative and inflammatory claims. A *New York Times* headline for January 15, 1996, read, "Now for the Bad News: A Teenage Timebomb." The article goes on to say, "They are just four, five and six years old now, but already they are making criminologists nervous." On May 9, 1996, a *USA Today* columnist cautioned that "the tsunami is coming.... Juvenile crime is going up and getting worse." During the same month, the *Tampa Tribune* wrote that these super-predators "are not some creature[s] from outer space; they are our own children," while the *Christian Science Monitor* declared that "America is being threatened by a growing cadre of cold blooded teens." Even the *Times* of London noted that the United States was burdened with children capable of "remorseless brutality."

Media broadcasts further reinforced these images of ruthless young criminals: of street "thugs"—mostly African American and Latino—being led away in handcuffs by police; of shopkeepers brutalized and terrorized by teenage robbers; of dark American streets cordoned off, dead bodies on the ground, and hoodie-wearing boys, arms cuffed behind their backs, sprawled against squad cars. All these images painted—and continue to paint—the collective portrait that most Americans cling to of a generation they believe threatens their very lives.

I remember reading and seeing those stories about the coming wave of youth crime about to crest and crash over the country, about the "wolf packs" of "super-predators" already breaking through society's barriers to menace our safe neighborhoods. The media's language with all its dire modifiers and gritty depictions were successful because, like everyone else, those stories—and "those kids"—scared *me*.

Until I remembered who those "super-predators" really were.

Until I remembered that every day I walked into a classroom full of the young men and women that the public thought of as dangerous criminals, gangsters who deserved to be locked up not only for what they *did*, but for what they *could* do, and *would* do given the chance.

Until I remembered that those kids' lives and even the crimes they committed—or were accused of committing—were far more complicated than the media industry ever reported or hinted at.

Once I realized what a powerful impact the media had had even on someone like me with my background and experience working with this population, I began to wonder how it affected the majority of people (a startling 76 percent, one communications professor at American University reported) who got their opinions about juvenile crime solely from what they read and saw on television.

One effect of this polemic against juvenile offenders was a public clamber for stiffer crime laws. Faced with these fear-fed demands, state and federal legislators jumped into the debate, mirroring and reinforcing the media's and the public's skewed perceptions and misconceptions.

In May 1996, U.S. Representative Bill McCollum of Florida introduced the Violent Youth Predator Act, its title reflecting the nation's grim attitude. During House deliberations, one representative warned, "Our youngest career criminals are getting away with the most heinous crimes over and over again. Wake up!" Another congressman proclaimed that "Americans are shocked by the brutality and viciousness of the crimes that are being committed by thirteen- and fourteen- and fifteen-year-olds, and they are equally shocked when they see a system that treats these juveniles as something less than the predators they seem to be."

A series of proposed bills moved through both houses of Congress, all with the message that juvenile offender laws on both the federal and state levels needed to be toughened, and toughened quickly.

States got the message. A majority, in one way or another, changed their laws to allow additional youths to be tried as adults. As Elizabeth Scott, a law professor at Columbia University, noted in the fall 2008 *Juvenile Justice*, these legal reforms "resulted in wholesale transfer of youths into the adult criminal system—more than 250,000 a year by most estimates." Young people who in every other way were legal minors were considered adults when it came to crime. Hooked on sound bites, the public and politicians called for "adult time for adult crime."

Many state laws also stripped away a variety of protective measures that in the past had guarded the confidentiality of juveniles who had gotten into trouble, thus taking away what slim chance they had of changing their lives and moving on. Some states diverted, and continue to divert, money from education into building more jails for these "super-predators." In many parts of the country building jails and keeping them filled—the "prison-industrial complex"—is now a crucial part of struggling local economies.

It was as if the whole culture—television and newspapers; politicians and policy makers; the general public—had conspired to lock these kids up, and once there, to make their lives as perilous as possible.

Even their own hip-hop culture appeared to work against them, glorifying and celebrating the very things that terrified mainstream America. Rap lyrics, music videos, movies, and magazines reinforced society's negative perception of teenagers—black teenagers, at that—as vicious street thugs who are only interested in money, sex, drugs, and the guns you needed to get, and to keep, all those things.

But how did this "super-predator" witch hunt translate on the ground?

The national mood confirmed local law enforcement's long held opinions that these kids were lawless, reckless, and dangerous. Backed by the public's fears and the politicians' renewed "get tough" stance, police stepped up their efforts against troubled teens and set out to clean up the streets.

Vincent Schiraldi, president of the Justice Policy Institute, called the 1990s a punishing decade for America "with nearly as many people added to our prisons and jails as in America's entire history prior to 1990." The PEW Charitable Trust's much discussed report "One in 100: Behind Bars in America 2008" confirmed this bleak view, stating that "three decades of growth in America's prison population has quietly nudged the nation across a sobering threshold: for the first time, more than one in every 100 adults is now confined in an American jail or prison." In 1990, on any given day, U.S. statistical reports show that there were over twenty-five hundred kids in jails; in 2007 that number had almost tripled to seven thousand.

No one who has taught in a jail in the last two decades would be surprised by either statement. As jailhouse teachers, we confronted these stark statistics every day. We knew that getting "tougher on crime" meant getting even tougher on young offenders.

In the county lockup where I taught, our classrooms were packed as local police swept through the most vulnerable neighborhoods arresting more and more kids, the vast majority of whom were poor, minority, and male (although there was also an alarming increase in the number of females arrested).

Busting young criminals made good politics. The county district attorney's office prided itself on its no compromise stance. Whatever crimes these youths were initially arrested for, the prosecutor slapped them with the most serious charges possible within that classification, charges that then warranted the harshest punishment. As a result, they received stiffer sentences from the courts. Minors who before might have gotten probation, community service, mandatory rehab, or short jail time, were looking at a year to two years in county lockup, while more and more were being sent to state prisons for long bids behind bars. Suddenly, kids in greater numbers were doomed to the world of incarceration, which they were far from equipped to navigate, let alone survive.

Anthony was one of those youngsters. He had been raised in a Yonkers long-term residential center. Although he was seventeen, he had the goofy body of a twelve-year-old and moved through the world with a twelve-year-old's awkwardness.

When, however, it came to him making decisions, taking responsibility, or staying out of trouble, Anthony was at an even greater handicap than his clumsiness. Mildly developmentally disabled, with no family to speak of, and an African American young male in a society where race matters, he spent his life stumbling in and out of sticky situations. Yet somehow he always managed to avoid the big trouble. There was a gentleness and innocence about him that appealed to people, even to the cops and judges he stood in front of a number of times for mischief of one kind or another. So, unlike many of his peers, Anthony had made it to seventeen with no criminal record.

But that wasn't the case when he walked into my basic education classroom in the county jail. Anthony was facing serious time in state prison for his part in a robbery. He had been with two other boys who snatched a purse from a woman—the wife of a local cop, of all things—at the county mall. As they were running away, the guy who had grabbed the purse tossed it to Anthony who was then caught by the police.

Anthony was culpable. He had done a dumb thing. This time his lack of judgment—and his lack of ability to make judgments—finally caught up with him. But it was even more serious than that. Anthony had been caught up in the war on crime, the war on kids in trouble.

There was talk of a gun that the boys denied having, there was talk of threats, and the DA's office charged all three with armed robbery. The prosecutor refused to plea bargain Anthony's case. He was sentenced to do state time. Despite the school social worker's efforts to get his sentence reduced, citing his clean record, his obvious mental and social deficiencies, and his incredible vulnerability in the predator-prey food chain of state prison, the sentence stuck, and Anthony, terrified for his life, was sent upstate.

But the jailhouse school wasn't filled with just Anthonys.

No one would deny that teens were committing crimes, some serious and disturbing. However, no one—on a national, state, or local level—made an effort to find ways to hold these young people accountable other than by locking them up. Nor did anyone tackle in any meaningful way the larger issues that made them failures at life—issues such as racism, the wide and widening gap between the haves and the have-nots, disintegrating families, and neighborhoods wrecked by violence, drugs, and disease. The whole juvenile justice system had gone from rehabilitation, which had always been its underpinning philosophy, to punishment.

The world that America created for its "super-predators" was desolate and bleak and severely damaging not only to them but also to their families, neighborhoods, towns, and our society at large. With jails overflowing and new high-tech prisons being built, even John Dilulio, as early as 1997, began to publicly distance himself from what was happening, saying in the *Wall Street Journal* that these young criminals "could not and should not be punished into submission."

Nevertheless, the county lockup where I taught and jails across the country were filled with young men and women: disaffected, disturbed, neglected, in need of medication but without medication, addicted to drugs, to alcohol—young people who society was punishing for victimizing others, yet who, at the same time, were well aware that society had never held anyone accountable for victimizing them over the years. Although the juvenile crime wave that John Dilulio predicted hasn't happened, the public still clings to its views of these teenagers as the enemy, a view so endemic to our culture that by now very few people can see the distortion.

Even as I watched all this unfold nationally, locally, and in my own jailhouse classroom, and saw how misinformation and prejudice shaped our country's thinking and actions, it took me a while before I began to see that I was just as much caught up in my own biases and judgments as the rest of the public.

From my first day at the jail, as I waited in the lobby to be cleared for security, watching the lobby officer treat the mostly women visitors as though they were the ones who had committed the crimes that put their loved ones in jail, I instantly knew whose side I was on. I knew who the "good guys" were and who the "bad" were; who were the "us" and who were the "them" in this labyrinthine power equation.

I was on the side of the mistreated visitors—the mothers and grandmothers; the young girlfriends, pregnant or already mother to "his seed"; the uncle, father, brother, or homeboy—the rare male not locked up. And I was on the side of the inmates: victims of a racist society; beat up, beat down by an unfair criminal justice system.

Maybe they *were* violent, nasty, cruel, and irresponsible—but all with good reason.

And I knew that anyone in the Department of Corrections was the enemy, the victimizer, the perpetrator, the exploiter, the bully.

At first, everything I saw and heard, and overheard, in this alien and at times frightening world cemented my ideas. Jail was proving to be jail.

It would be some time before my certainties about the people I worked with—students and correctional officers, or COs—would shift and change the way everything else did in prison culture. Despite its firm foundations in stone and steel, in locks and razor wire, jail, although designed to control uncontrollable chaos, is a place of constant change and uncertainty. Inmates were transferred from block to block for seemingly arbitrary reasons; officers were shifted to different assignments; codes blared over the PA system and all of a sudden there was "no movement," and a floor, a block, the whole prison was on lockdown. Even within my day I moved around to various parts of the facility, teaching different groups in different classrooms, changes dictated not just by academic needs, but by the demands of the Department of Corrections.

But the longer I worked there, the more I realized that jail had gotten me the way it did everyone else who spends any time behind bars—COs and wardens, nurses and doctors, kitchen workers and maintenance guys, the inmates I taught and the people who came to visit them: I was taking sides just like everybody else in a system that demanded it, that thrived on distinctions and encampments; on rifts and ranks; on factions and divisions. I was taking sides like every other American in a culture, in a society, in a nation that thrived on the same divide of "us" and "them."

It became clear to me that the war on youth crime affected not only the young people trapped in the system, but also the men and women who worked in the county lockup week in and week out, some for sixteen hours a day. Once I got to know the COs and heard their stories, I saw that the problems these locked up kids wrestled with—economic hardship, drugs and alcohol, abandonment, abuse, family stress—weren't really much different from the issues that the COs faced in their own lives.

Until finally I understood that their struggles—locked up kids and correctional staff alike—were much like the challenges that all the rest of us living outside those razor-wired fences dealt with in one way or another. Suddenly worlds I once confidently thought were completely removed from each other—and from me and the rest of America—shared a common ground.

I Don't Wish Nobody to Have a Life Like Mine: Tales of Kids in Adult Lockup tells the stories of the men and women—inmate, uniformed staff, and civilian—who moved in and out of the county lockup during my ten years there. Some were there for only weeks, some for months, others for years. Yet each of their stories helped me erode and finally cross the line in the sand I resolutely drew between "us" and "them" that first day in the visitors' lobby.

Ultimately, each of their stories has the power to help all of us realize that there really is no line to erode, no line to cross, that all the divisions we are quick to define, all the barriers we are quick to put up—of the haves and have-nots; of the keepers and the kept; of the right and wrong, the good and bad—are no more substantial than the sand itself we Americans are so ready to draw a line through.

Chapter One

The Human Stain

I hate civilians," Warden Clooney barked into the microphone. He stood as close to the podium as his huge stomach let him and scanned his audience. We were all civilians, and we were all there for new employee orientation.

It was my first week of teaching high school in what would turn out to be over a ten-year bid at Westchester County Correctional Facility.

I'd taught "at-risk" teenagers for thirteen years before that. But I was about to find out that the kids who would make their way into my various jailhouse classrooms throughout my day and over my years there weren't "at-risk" anymore. They *were* risk—to themselves, to their families, to their girlfriends, to their enemies, to the towns they lived in, to the whole goddamn society.

At least that would be Warden Clooney's take on things.

I groaned when my supervisor, Rose, told me that I had to attend an orientation. She was a middle-aged woman who, despite her delicate name and fine linen suits, walked the minor blocks—notorious for their fights and fist-size water bugs—with the gruffness of any seasoned prison guard.

"I know, I know," she said.

"Waste of time. But look at it this way. You'll get to see corrections at its finest." She laughed. "As if you haven't already. All you have to do is spend a day here and you've seen enough. But you still have to go. It's over in the training academy."

The academy was housed in a low building just behind the newer high-tech jail, a stack of five-story, beige, stone blocks and blue ceramic borders. The academy's soot-colored brick looked like it had been around since 1914 when the older part of the jail first opened as a work farm.

Back then, inmates spent long days tending vegetables sold to local markets and milking the cows that roamed the fields, which now were paved over for parking lots.

Back then, the county lockup was idyllically called Grasslands, situated in the hamlet of Valhalla.

But nobody was fooled by those bucolic names, then or now. Not even the kids I taught, who were locked up for everything from trespassing to murder, and who were firmly locked into the twenty-first century.

Even they knew the time-honored rumors about Grasslands. It was as though the inmates had their own orientation for new jacks where the jail legends were passed down from generation to generation: how in the old days, before razor wire spooled for miles around the place, a runaway would be sniffed down by dogs howling across the cattle fields all the way to the Hudson, or how prisoners were beaten to death, then secretly buried behind the corn rows.

"That's why they call the town, Valhalla, Mr. C," Thunder announced with great authority the day I started a lesson on mythology.

He was a blond hayseed from Peekskill, a rural town up-county that was no stranger to cows or murders, who was doing time for what he called a "bogus drug charge."

Thunder was really Olaf.

He was named after his Norse grandfather, but he insisted on everyone calling him Thunder.

"You know, like Thor? The god of thunder?" he graciously explained to me.

He swore that he was proud of his birth name, but I suspected it just called down too much misery on him, so Thunder it was.

It was that same Grandfather Olaf who taught him the old stories about the Norse gods when he was a little kid.

"Valhalla was the graveyard of slain warriors," he said, lowering his voice as though in reverence for all the valiantly killed Viking fighters—or runaway inmates. Plus it helped not to let the "po-lice" hear anything you said.

The inside of the academy was as dark and gloomy as any tomb for the real or imagined dead. Its windows were covered by tinny grates, as though the sun itself was just another contraband item to be kept out.

The room where we met looked like the basement cafeteria of my old grade school with the same chipped linoleum and long lunch tables. Up front were a blackboard and a battered wooden podium.

Twenty of us sat along those tables, all civilians, all professionals of one kind or another—teachers, medical staff, mental health counselors, law librarians.

No one said anything, as though we were in detention for some particularly despicable offense. Instead we sipped lukewarm coffee, shuffled through the papers we were required to sign showing we had received them, shifted on the uncomfortable collapsible metal chairs, all the while trying to look at the ID tags that hung around each of our necks.

We weren't so much interested in names at that point; that would come later when, in our endless struggle as service providers to get something done through the muddle of corrections' bureaucracy, we'd form our own conspiracy of courtesy.

What seemed important then was to figure out what each of us did, to define the terms of our turf. It turned out to be impossible since the names of the organizations each of us worked for were encrypted in a scramble of acronyms.

But it didn't matter; the mystery was cleared up by Warden Clooney from the very beginning: we were all civilians, so we were the enemy.

"As far as I'm concerned, civilians just get in the way, especially nurses. We got any nurses here today?" he glared across his audience.

Of course, no one raised their hands.

Instead, we all leaned closer to the table pretending to eagerly catch every word the man had to say, inadvertently, of course, covering up our IDs. You never knew, maybe your group would be next on his hit list of contempt.

"Nurses are a bunch of knee-jerk liberals, always making trouble over some 'poor inmate.'" He spit this last phrase out like a gob of sour tobacco juice.

That morning, though, Warden Folk had clearly drawn the line and we all knew, or thought we knew, who *us* and *them* were.

"I'm finally retiring after thirty years, getting out of this shit hole, so now I can say anything I want," he growled, looking from face to face for a challenge.

It was hard to believe that last remark since I got the impression that nothing had ever stopped him before from saying exactly what he felt like saying.

"In all the years I been in the Department of Corrections, I've never seen anybody 'corrected,' not a goddamn one.

"All human garbage.

"I don't care what they're in here for. I've seen it all. Kids robbin' old ladies for their social security checks, crackheads selling their babies, punk college boys in for drunk driving. And some of you might remember that dentist in '94, killed his wife and put her through the wood chipper?" He hit his chest as though he had something to do with the man's conviction.

"Garbage, every last one of them.

"The sooner you learn that the better.

"And they'll charm the pants off you. . . . I've seen that, too."

It took me a second to figure out he was laughing. His thick, white neck got red, he sipped water to catch his breath, sputtered, choked on it, tugged at his collar, pulled on his tie, and mopped his face with a handkerchief.

"Bet you wish there was one of those knee-jerk liberal nurses in the audience now," I thought to myself as the man looked as though his face would explode.

But he was clearly enjoying himself.

He had spent his career insulting captive audiences of one kind or another. The fact that we were professionals and had greater scope to be outraged obviously made it more fun for him.

"Never forget that you're dealing with the common criminal. They're not all toothless winos checked in for 'a cot and three hots.'

"Some of them talk real pretty, *real pretty*, ed-u-cated, suave, innocent—well, of course, they're *all* innocent."

Again, that redneck wheeze of a laugh.

"But they're all scum, bags of garbage who'll rip you off in a heartbeat. So let me give you some tips.

"Don't tell them where you live. Obvious, right? But you'd be surprised.

"Oh, yeah, and something else, you know, how, in your car? Sometimes you leave stuff on the seat? Maybe a magazine or some mail? Cover it up, because we got work crews roaming around the place, suppose to be cleared for outside duties, the 're-hab-bilitated' ones, but they'll rob you blind when they get out, or call and tell their friends to pay your place a visit while you're at work here.

"And don't give them anything, no food, no candy, not even a Halls cough drop; next thing you know, they'll start extorting you, get you to bring in other stuff.

"I know, I know. You're sitting there thinking, 'This guy's nuts. I wouldn't do something so stupid like that.' But I tell you, I've seen it all. Cigarettes, new sneakers, weed, pills, porno, even fried chicken."

He leaned on the podium and scanned his audience. Slowly he shook his head as though he genuinely felt sorry for us, this pathetic bunch of losers.

Then, as if to confirm this impression, he went on.

"Now, I'm going to tell you how to save your life.

"There hasn't been a riot here since 1981. But when you're dealing with human garbage, you never know. Let me tell you what you're supposed to do if they take you hostage."

Suddenly, Warden Clooney had everyone's attention.

I suspect that his preferred approach to any riot or hostage takeover would be just to blow everybody away, criminals, hostages, the whole bunch of them; just get rid of them. They shouldn't have gotten themselves into the situation to begin with.

Still, he did give us some practical hints.

"First thing you do is get rid of your ID, just toss it. If you're lucky the department won't charge you the twenty-five bucks for losing it."

Another one of his jokes.

This time at least a few people in the audience gave a nervous giggle.

"If you got a tie on or a white coat for you medical types, take it off. Don't look official. You want to blend into the concrete. Don't try to make peace or get on your high horse and be the spokesman for the inmates.

"And we certainly don't need *you* talking to the scumbags for *us*; we got state guys get big bucks for that shit.

"If it gets nasty, and we have to go in, well, you don't want to know. Just don't watch, and hope you get to *not* tell what you *didn't* see. If you get my drift."

Nobody even gave a polite smile.

"And I'm here to tell you, they'll come at you with anything, they got all kinds of homemade weapons," he said.

Then, to prove his point, he hefted a big cardboard box onto the table.

One by one, Warden Clooney pulled out weapons that inmates had made out of all kinds of things and that DOC had confiscated on their periodic shakedowns.

He waved them around like a barker at a freak show hawking his wares of perversity, of nature turned against itself: the two-headed baby, the hairy ape woman, the perfect circle of the snake that ate itself.

But in this case, it was a bright blue toothbrush handle honed down to a sharp point; a bar of state soap tightly wrapped in a T-shirt made to fit a fist like a brass knuckle; a white sock filled with batteries; a Pepsi can torn in half, its edges serrated, ready to rake across some enemy's face.

"And you know where they get *these*, don't you?" he said, glaring at me, the only teacher in the audience, as he held up a dozen paper clips straightened out and taped together, and a pencil without its eraser, its metal top pinched closed and sharpened to a razor thinness.

Each object had its own story.

As Warden Clooney held up one makeshift weapon after another, he told us how it was made, how it had been used, and how it had been found. The hiding places for some of these weapons were as ingenious as their construction: inside a showerhead, the hollowed leg of a bunk bed, buried in a pail of laundry detergent. And we heard about ears cut off, faces slashed, backs and chests scarred, jaws broken.

"Ya see this? It's a telephone receiver, right?

"Some piece of crap ripped this outta of the wall. Ripped—it—outta—the god—damn wall, and smashed in some poor CO's skull."

He held it out toward us, urging us to take it, pass it around between us like exhibit A in a courtroom.

But no one made a move to take it. No one even looked up at it.

We all knew that we were the ones on trial, that he was looking for the perfect fit: not the grasping hand or smudged fingerprints, but the look of sad compassion, the look that said, "Oh, those poor inmates, driven to such violence and despair."

It's because of people like you, his mad-eyed glower accused, that this kind of thing happens. Knee-jerk liberals, pro-fessionals, service-providers, coming in here and throwing off the natural order of things.

"And you wantta know *why* that scumbag did it?

"Because the poor bastard of a CO was just telling him to get off the phone for the tenth time so other friggin' inmates could use the phone to call their families."

With a final air of triumph, he held the shiny black phone receiver over his head and waved it at us like a huge thighbone caked with blood and hanks of scalp, his smirk saying it all. "Every last one of them, human garbage."

By then we were all embarrassed, staring down at the table in front of us.

We were embarrassed for Warden Clooney and the waste of all his years here.

We were embarrassed for the officers and inmates, the keepers and the kept, whose day-to-day struggles had been exposed so cavalierly, supposedly for our edification.

We were embarrassed for ourselves sitting there silently, not challenging Warden Clooney, not standing up to him.

But finally we were embarrassed for working in this graveyard of slain warriors and for being a part of this great human garbage heap called life.

"Well, you're not gettin' paid to eat our doughnuts and drink our coffee. You all got jobs to do," he said as though he'd read our thoughts.

"Anybody have any questions?" he asked as he pushed himself away from the podium, patting his paunch as though he'd just eaten a good meal.

"I didn't think so," he snickered. "Well then, you good people have a *great* day."

Chapter Two

From the Projects to the Condos

L eading into the old jail building was a heavy, wooden, cathedral-like door with a marble banner arched over it. It was hard to read the inscription chiseled into the stone since some of the words had been eroded by decades of weather.

There were two things, though, I could make out on that stone scroll: "Grasslands Work Farm" and "Est. 1914." Whatever else that inscription might have said—there was a blurred something or other about "haven," "repent," "rest"—it was pretty clear that they meant business inside those castellated walls built by immigrant masons fresh from the faraway hills of Italy.

Every morning on my way into the building where my classroom was for the first few years I taught in the county lockup, I had to walk through a blue-hazed huddle of COs standing in that doorway desperately trying to smoke themselves into tranquility before they faced their next shift.

It didn't matter that I knew most of the men hunched together there, that I saw them day in and day out in the halls or on the blocks. They still ignored me, the way COs did whenever they got together and civilian staff was around.

Even so, I still held a set smile as I weaved my way through that cloud of smoke.

If I happened to catch O'Shay's or Brink's eye, the officers I worked with, I'd nod, even though I knew they couldn't acknowledge me.

Instead, they'd shuffle in closer to that uniformed center of gravity, look away, then tilt their heads up and blow smoke into the sky.

Once I had slipped through that silent knot, I'd push the door open.

You didn't expect to find that kind of entranceway at the county work farm. It was opulent with polished slate floors, carved mahogany wainscoting, and a black lacquered counter where boxes and packages were received, and where I had my schoolbag searched every morning.

Nailed on the wall behind the counter was a large cherrywood panel with the Department of Corrections' mission statement meticulously but crudely burned into it.

I never got to read it through.

I was too busy dodging the verbal bullets that Officer Daven, the security officer assigned to that post, directed at all us unarmed civilians.

"Twenty. Friggin'. Years. That's how long I been doing this post for, and all I got left is five more. Then I'm out of this shit hole," Daven would bark at me as though I was the one keeping him locked up behind that counter, his big, red face pinking up to the top of his balding head.

"But I'll get me a friggin' good pension at forty-six, and do the volunteer fireman thing full time.

"That is if these goddamn allergies don't knock me out completely." He'd close his eyes, rub his temples, and grimace.

"But the bitch"—that's what he called his girlfriend; he said it with an eye cocked for your reaction. If you gave a disapproving glance, or tightened your jaw trying not to say anything, or made even the slightest turn away, you were guaranteed to stand there even longer than usual waiting for him to unlock the door—"she's got me on some new herbal shit that seems to be working."

For people he held in such contempt, Officer Daven told us civilians an awful lot about himself. How he'd slept; what he ate the night before; how much he had had to drink and shouldn't have had; the eternal condition of his sinuses, his back, his bowels.

He complained and snarled and sniped.

He didn't care how many times you shifted from foot to foot, tossed your backpack to the other shoulder, or shuffled toward the door that lead into the jail, anxious to get to work.

After all, what the hell did he care?

He was already at his friggin' job.

He had nothing else to do.

So, he'd finish an article in the *Daily News*, or read parts of it to you, or worse yet, want to discuss it with you even though you didn't know what it was about.

Or he had to sort the mail or just stare the other way.

He did it all so methodically, so routinely, it made you think it was all a part of the jail's standard operating procedures.

When he finally got around to searching my schoolbag, things didn't move any faster.

"Why you got all these pens?" he'd ask, holding up the felt-tips like they were smuggled switchblades.

"What are you gonna do with them rulers? They'll only steal them on you and then Warden Foreman will kick your butt out of a job." He'd chuckle.

"Tums? Tums? You know you can't have them in here. They're drugs, for chrissake."

Then, as though it wasn't fun anymore, he'd shake his head in disgust, amble from behind the counter, and unlock the door.

Once Daven slammed that inner door behind you, though, there was another surprise.

You found yourself in an enclosed courtyard with a flagstone walkway connecting the front entrance to the jail. It was lined with ferns, flowers, and well-groomed shrubs. The small strip of lawn behind the flower borders was close cut and green.

But things were a lot different inside the old jail building.

The floors were gouged and discolored linoleum or just bare concrete. They still carried a high sheen; the inmates saw to that, spending hours polishing them. Nowhere else except in America's jails will you see bare concrete waxed and buffed.

The burnished floors didn't make up for the cracked cement walls, stained brown from the leaking, swayed-back roof. The tall windows were permanently fogged, and the light coming through them was murky. The bars covering the windows were mottled with layers of old chipped paint. And it didn't matter what time of day it was, there was always the smell of rancid cole slaw.

Walking those decayed hallways you realized that the grand stonework front, that entranceway with its polished wood and slate, and that manicured courtyard were all a façade and what that word suggested: a pose, a front, a cover-up for this warehouse for human beings.

It was easy to see why my students called the jail "the projects." Most of them had grown up in public housing, those other warehouses of human misery, where home was made of cracked concrete, pocked by random gunshots. Windows were broken and stayed that way, and metal doors were dented, kicked in by the cops, kids, or rival drug dealers. The paint didn't peel because it had long ago blistered, curled up, and disintegrated, that is, if there had ever been any paint.

After I wended my way down the corridors, dodging random drips or navigating the slalom of plastic garbage cans dotted around to catch water even on dry days, I still had to walk through B block to get to my classroom.

Morning was a busy time for a block officer, so I'd have to wait outside the gate as CO Gomez slowly and deliberately made his tour of the cells before he let me in.

As the stifling heat of the block and the stench of unwashed bodies and county-issued orange uniforms funneled toward me, I was aware that I was standing on the threshold of the home of thirty men.

But even though I was uninvited, I was always welcomed.

The inmates who lived along that long, low ceilinged hall would look up from brushing their teeth at their shoe-box-size sinks, or from reading their bibles or Korans while hunched on their rumpled bunks to greet me. They'd nod, smile, and call out that great honorific for all jailhouse educators, "Morning, Teach."

There would be the same guy, black as a new tarred road, doing his five hundred push-ups in the middle of the block hallway at exactly seven thirty every morning, his perpetually pumped-up biceps glistening with sweat. He never interrupted his count as I walked around him, but he always tilted his head and gave me a wide gaped-tooth smile.

And Parsons who, despite the fact that he always kept his face turned toward the back of his cell, somehow knew when I was going by and would call out over his bony, stooped shoulder scraped clean by heroin, "You have a good one, there, Mr. Teach," waving to the wall.

Or the card players who'd be in the exact same spot where I left them the night before when I went home for the day. They'd be slapping down the same cards on the same square of floor, cursing their same bad luck, calling out the same "You take care now." Every once in a while, one of them would look up and shake his close-shaved head and give me a wry smile, as though to say, "Can you believe it? Another day in this shit hole."

Some of the old-timers, men beaten up by booze and by the bankrupt life it made for them, would stop their shuffle on the way to the showers and ask me in confidential tones, "How the young ones doin'?"

Then, they'd preach to the choir. They'd tell me how important education was, that if *they* had just stayed in school, listened to their teachers, their mamas, they wouldn't be standing there, a whole lifetime wasted in and out of lockup.

Officer Gomez liked to walk me down the hall to my classroom door. It wasn't that he was afraid anything would happen to me. Word had it around the jail that despite his stubby stature, pudgy features, and lisp he ran a tight block. In all the years he'd been on B block, there'd never been a code called.

But he didn't maintain control the way a lot of the other COs did. He didn't snarl, or bully, or threaten. He didn't listen to gossip or set one inmate against the other.

Instead, he walked the block, listened to the men. He knew when to laugh at somebody's bluster and when to take it seriously. He kept an eye on things, and always fought to make sure the guys got what few privileges and supplies were due to them from DOC. The men liked and respected him for that. They even pretended not to hear his lisp, which sounded downright cartoonish coming out of this chubby little guy with the fat lips.

I knew Gomez took that walk because he liked to complain.

He complained about the hard life he and his fellow gatekeepers led. I'd hear about the needless paperwork to be filed; or the endless bickering with the supplies department about the linens or toilet paper that his men didn't get and that supplies claimed they had sent up; or the rings he was mandated to punch in on the security phone every fifteen minutes to show he was patrolling the block.

"Some poor guy could be 'hanging up,'" he'd repeat every morning, his lisp more pronounced the more excited he got. "He could be dangling by his neck in his cell and them assholes in administration would expect me to stop from cutting him down to do my rings."

He always ended up laughing, though, at his own predictability or at my usual noncommittal but sympathetic nod, or at his lack of sibilance, or maybe at the whole friggin' mess.

Then, just before he closed and locked the classroom door behind me, he'd say, "Anything you need, you just tell me. You know them in headquarters don't give a shit about nobody."

Conditions weren't much different in my classroom. The ceilings and walls were cracked and stained. I had to move equipment around to dodge the unpredictable ceiling drips. The chalkboard was as pocked and gouged as the linoleum, and in places it was impossible to write on.

Jails are pretty porous places despite their metal and stone, so sounds and smells seeped in. My days were punctuated by the constant clatter of gates slamming and a steady stream of jailhouse invectives spouted by inmates and COs alike. And the soupy stench of hundreds of men living together and of carts of leftover food trays abandoned in hallways leaked in.

Then, after a couple years of Daven's daily assaults and Gomez's grumbles, of leaks and smells, of muddy light and blaring noise, I was assigned—at least for a while, since where I taught was switched as much as where the inmates were housed, moved from block to block—to another classroom in what was still called "the new jail," even though it was constructed in 1992, several years before I came there. A multimillion dollar building, it could hold even more prisoners, and hold them more efficiently.

"Wooee, Mr. C, moving up in the world," some of the guys and not a few COs teased. "Goin' to the condos."

The new jail wasn't anything like its older counterpart. It had double doors that automatically opened at your approach. There was a designated smoking area far from the entrance. The reception area was spacious and flushed with light from a front wall of frosted glass stretching from floor to ceiling, and the air inside was cool and fresh and antiseptic.

Security was still security, but now we civilians were greeted politely, and quickly cleared through a metal detector. If you happened to be pinned to the spot by the detector's insistent bleatings—a belt buckle, the unseen steel toes of your shoes—the officers apologetically asked you to step back, to remove your belt, or to take your shoes off—then quickly sent you on your way.

Once inside the main building, a faceless force behind tinted windows in a central control bubble opened gates electronically. You knew you were still being watched because every once in a while, an anonymous voice would boom out over the PA system.

"Excuse me, sir, excuse me. Please display your ID."

You weren't exactly sure who the voice was talking to. At the sound of that command, all we civilians would look around nervously the way people in a busy store do, reaching for their cell phones not sure if that familiar ring is for them or not.

There was still the sound of glass and steel gates sliding open and shut, but it was more muffled and measured.

And although inmates continued to move through the halls that spidered out from the center core to clinics and visiting rooms, they were always escorted by an officer and under the stern stare of other COs posted along the way to monitor everyone's movement.

Unlike the blocks in the old jail, the new facility's housing units were cleaner, more spacious, and air-conditioned. Each inmate had his own cell. Although it was stripped down to penal basics of bunk, sink, and toilet, there were walls instead of bars and a windowed door that could be shut. The men shared a common area for eating, watching TV, or playing cards.

Still, there were the usual fights, the same yelling and cursing, the same occasional food tray flung across the dayroom, the same Monopoly board flipped over, and the perennial battles between the men and COs.

My classroom was on the second floor, the first floor of inmate housing. Unlike my old classroom where I felt like a coal miner trapped in a dark airless pit, I had a large glass window that opened onto the hallway and flooded the room with light.

The walls were solid, painted a soothing cream. The only thing I had to use my wastebasket for was paper and pencil shavings since the ceiling was acoustic tile and dry.

Suddenly, I had bookshelves, worktables, study carrels, a dazzling white dry board, and bulletin boards to hang up maps and posters.

Of course, there was still movement.

There's always movement in a jail.

Right after breakfast and right after lunch, a nurse would push her medication cart past to the glass-gated sally port where the inmates—adults and kids alike—lined up waiting for their meds.

If I was lucky the nurse would be someone who respected the guys' privacy and was willing to stoop down and talk through the metal grate used for passing medications.

Most nurses, though, just yelled past the glass. More often than not, their tone was impatient because some inmate questioned a change that had been made in his medication and that he hadn't been told about, or complained that he hadn't been seen by the dentist yet, even though he'd put in a sick call slip over a week ago.

I ended up hearing more about these men's medical conditions—who had AIDS or rotting teeth or clap or hemorrhoids—then I wanted to know, or should have known.

Four mornings a week, a group of men were herded past my window into the elevator on their way to county court. It was an odd mix of scruffy and well-groomed.

Some inmates made the trip with their hair tangled in a nest of knots and their orange scrubs dirty and wrinkled, while others had close-cropped hair and shaved faces fresh from the barber's clippers, their oranges pressed as though they had been just picked up from the dry cleaners.

They all shared, though, that same glum, beaten-down look of men going to meet The Man.

And once a week, two trusties with a CO escort would push huge carts of fresh linen into the hallway. The officer in central control would announce over the PA system in a hotel lobby voice you could actually understand, "Linen exchange, gentlemen, linen exchange."

These distractions played across the screen of the classroom's clear glass window. They'd interrupt whatever was going on during class. Not that many of the kids to whom I was trying to explain the difference between an adverb and an adjective, or a simple sentence and a complex sentence, wanted to listen to me, anyway.

It didn't take much to get them going.

"There's that bitch nurse who won't give me nothing for my toof," Mikal would complain, looking up from the morning's writing assignment, his hand cupping his jaw, his rotting molars as much a source of pain as his constantly postponed court dates.

"Shit, man, how come Bronx gets a trusty job and not me," Glen might gripe right in the middle of our reading when he sees his buddy sweeping the floor outside the window, not mentioning his four disciplinary lockdowns for having weed.

And there was always a chorus of moans and groans and catcalls when a female CO walked by.

"Yo, man, look at the butt on that one."

"Fuck, she's thick."

"She wants it."

With each distraction their heads bobbed up and down.

The only thing that stopped them from plastering themselves against the window like little boys kept in at recess was the CO assigned to the second floor hallway.

If an officer happened to hear their rumblings, the CO would glare in or push the door open and threaten.

"If you don't want to find your raggedy asses in twenty-three-hour lockdown, sit down and shut up." And just like that the room would freeze.

Despite the solid concrete (although even that began to crack soon enough with shoddy construction), new paint, and technology, it quickly became obvious that things for these locked-up boys in the new jail weren't that different from their buddies in the old jail. Just like anywhere else in the facility, they were still treated like the human garbage Warden Clooney drummed into our heads that first week in civilian orientation—although some COs didn't bother with the "human" part.

But after a few weeks I began to feel as though something was missing.

I certainly didn't miss the clouds of cigarette smoke, or the long traipse through the old jail's dirty hallways, or the noxious smells, or the constant noise, or the threats of violence and chaos.

It took me a while, but I finally realized that what I really missed was Daven and Gomez.

I missed their moans and groans, their bad moods, and their good moods. I missed being ignored, and I missed being held hostage to some endless story or complaint.

I kept wondering if Daven's girlfriend's herbal potion was still working, or if he had finally given up drinking like the doctor told him to.

And I wanted to know if Gomez ever got the extra linen he'd been battling for, or if he managed to stash away the toilet paper he was plotting to get so when the supplies department fucked him over one more time his men wouldn't be caught short.

Walking up the tree-shaded sidewalk in the morning, through the automatic doors, under the gaze of an invisible CO, I tried to imagine Daven and Gomez in this brave new world.

But I couldn't.

I knew that those two crusty old veterans, born and bred in the stench and clamor of the old jail hood, could never make it in the antiseptic, rule-bound condos.

Chapter Three

Prison Birthday

I'll do it like a graph."

It was Ray's twenty-first birthday and it was his life he was about to plot out like a mathematical problem.

I'd learned enough about Ray in the six months he had been in my classroom to know what his graph would look like. It was pretty much a downward trend.

Still, it was his twenty-first birthday, and happily all Ray saw was the blank white paper in front of him.

Hunched over the desk, he carefully drew his grid. Looking down at him I could see a small knot of scaly flesh nested in his curly black hair. I knew how much he hated that cyst. I'd sat by helplessly as he fingered it, picked at it, cursed it.

"It's why I'm crazy. It's growing into my brain," he'd wail.

Tumor, demons, drug residue. Everybody in the jail had ideas about how this wild-eyed, sandalwood-complected Puerto Rican got to be the way he was.

But whatever theories people put out, there was one fact no one debated. The boy *was* crazy.

Some mornings, coming into school after sixteen hours on the blocks, Ray's eyes fired off in all directions like newly pointed spark plugs. He'd pace and angrily mutter. Those days he was privy to a plot to overthrow the government, and preached against celebrating Christmas because "Santa Claus was really 'Satan's Claws,' get it?"

Most of my other students were able to leave the chaos of the cells behind when they came to school.

But not Ray.

Some days the brutality rose up from him like smoke from that hellfire. While other days, he was Lazarus stumbling back from the dead, eyes stabbed by the light.

Then he'd stand alone, haunted by what he saw the long night before: some skinny white boy beaten up for his supply of instant soups, or a sudden plague of cockroaches as big as fists. Some days he'd smell of shit and piss—jail weapons—hoarded, then flung at whatever demon some prisoner most feared—a CO, another locked-away kid, the devil himself. Ray witnessed it all and carried it with him.

But this morning was Ray's twenty-first birthday and birthdays are important if you're young and locked up.

I'd heard so many young kids in prison predict their own early deaths, that having any birthday comes as a surprise. This fatalism wasn't abstract nihilism, though. It was just brutal reality, *their* reality.

Over the years more than one student had described to me what it felt like to hold a friend or older brother as he slowly bled to death from a gunshot or knife wound, and to feel the warm blood seep down through his jeans into his own skin.

So here was whacked out Ray, making it to the ripe old age of twenty-one. And from the whispers I overheard, the night before had treated him well.

Cigarettes were long banned from the county lockup. But in Ray's honor a few butts got passed around, savored like a fine wine. There was some of that, too, home-brewed hooch concocted through the alchemy of sugar, bread, and rotting fruit. But even though someone thought enough of him to share his wine cellar, Ray was more touched by the guy who shared a bag of Oreos with him.

"I don't got nobody to put money on my books," he sheepishly explained to me. "So this dude, a white guy I hardly know, gives me a whole bag of Oreos. Just for me. But they're gone. We wolfed them down, the whole bunch of us."

Ray's rare toothy smile told me that this day was clearly his.

"Sometimes I feel that being born was my fault," he almost chanted as he started his tale.

He had the facts at his fingertips, down to the days, months, and years so he didn't hesitate. His pencil marked the axis with a steady flow of black, gritty hatch marks.

Even though he claimed, as he plotted his life, "I don't blame nobody but myself," I got the feeling Ray was keeping track in the faraway hope of some day settling the score.

"I was taken from my mother when I was five years old and never seen her again."

Ray pointed to an extra thick black line with a month, day, and year under it. It looked like a cross on a cemetery plot.

"My pops was already out of the picture. He was doin' his first long bid up in Attica." Ray sighed.

There was none of that pity in his voice when he talked about his mother.

"She was really messed up on drugs. That's when I started going to different foster homes. I was afraid a lot because I didn't know what was happening to me. A lot of them I was in were bad and you had to fight and be tough," Ray said, defending himself.

So as he got older his stays with foster families grew shorter and shorter.

I could hear the doors slamming on his back as the people he was placed with sent him packing, back to child welfare.

Eventually, even the courts decided that Ray wasn't fit for any kind of family life. They started placing him in various state detention centers.

"I was raped," Ray said, pointing to another blacker, thicker line. "Here."

The name of the institution was in all capital letters, again with a month, day, and year.

He didn't give me time to do the math. He did it for me.

"I was eleven. He was nineteen."

He shrugged.

After that there were suicide attempts, psychiatric hospitalizations, and drug rehabs because by that time Ray's genetic inheritance from his mother had kicked in.

"Everywhere I went people treated me like I was nobody because I didn't have a family."

But that changed when Ray turned fourteen, or so he'd hoped.

"That summer me and my man, Marcos, were living in abandoned cars, we was sick of getting locked up in those j.d. places. My pops had finished his bid by then and he came down to the Bronx looking for me.

"And," Ray crowed, "he found me!"

With his father came an instant family.

Suddenly aunts, and uncles, and cousins recognized him, the same people who'd spit on him when he was doing some low-key panhandling.

Now they proclaimed him as one of their own, giving his name its full Spanish flourish, Reynaldo! They opened their homes to him, they fed him, they invited him to family picnics after Sunday mass.

Ah, he was home at last!

Well, at least while his father was around.

"Deep down they never did think of me like *real* family. Once my pops left it didn't take long for them to be like everybody else. He had to get out. The Yonkers po-lice hated him."

It sounded convincing the way Ray said it. But he still looked like that five-year-old suddenly bereft all over again.

"I lived with my Aunt Sally for a while."

He drew a circle around her name on the grid and blackened a point in the center. Target practice.

"I think my pops gave her money to let me live there," Ray went on.

"Money or no money, she used to lock me up at night with a bucket to piss in and a pitcher of water to drink," he said, darkening that bull's-eye.

"It hurt me for my own aunt to treat me like that."

Even that treatment came to an end.

A few days before Christmas, she kicked him out. But she didn't abandon him altogether. She got his SSI checks and cashed them.

"I was back sleeping on the streets. But one night this Puerto Rican drug dealer felt sorry for me sitting in the cold, so he tells me to come over to his apartment and he'd give me a winter coat."

Ray's eyes shone the way they did when he talked about his father.

"He believed in helping his peoples, and he believed in God," he added.

Maybe so, because that same night Ray moved in with this Puerto Rican drug dealer (that was the only way Ray talked about him), his wife, Rosa, and their five-year-old son, Joey.

That first night Joey sat and stared at him as Ray drank a cup of hot tea. He giggled when Ray put in lots of sugar and milk. He hadn't eaten in days. Ray blushed, especially after Rosa used her son's name "Joey" as a warning.

Then, as though to apologize, Joey grabbed his hand and pulled him into his bedroom. It was a pleasure palace stuffed with toys and high-tech gadgets.

But Joey hadn't brought him in to look at any of that. Instead, he sat his new friend on his bed and walked over to the toy cabinet. He took something from the bottom shelf, then cupped whatever it was in both his hands as though he was afraid it would escape. The little boy told Ray to put his hands together. Then, Joey dropped a small, perfectly round rock into Ray's creased and dirty palms.

"I'd never seen anything like it before," Ray remembered.

He put the pencil down and cupped his hands as though to give me the memory. "It was pink and all around it was a really thin black line."

Joey's grandfather gave him that rock when they visited him on his farm in Puerto Rico.

Soon after their visit, his grandfather died and it became Joey's lucky rock. From then on whenever his father went "out to work" he put it in his son's hands and told him to hold on to it until he came home safely.

But that didn't stop Joey from insisting that Ray take the rock.

"You keep it, okay?" Joey said to him that first evening. "You keep it and it will keep you, and Papa and Mamita, and me safe."

After that the two were inseparable, and they played their hearts out.

Ray knew what going "out to work" meant for his patron. So he kept Joey away from certain corners and neighborhoods. Even so, shopkeepers called out to Joey. Men in black Lexuses with gold trim waved to the boy. But Ray kept him walking.

"Joey was always saying he wanted to be like me." Ray shook his head in bewilderment. "But inside I kept saying, 'You don't want to be like me, little bro. You want to be better than me. I'm nobody. Nobody.'"

But every day of the three months that Ray lived with his new family, he began to see the possibility of finally being somebody, if only as a reflection in Joey's worshipful gaze.

But eventually even that reflection shattered.

"Last April"—another black cross on Ray's lifeline—"Joey's father asked me to give some papers to his lawyer. He never asked me to do anything for him, so I did," Ray said. "I waited all afternoon at his office but the guy never showed."

It was late when Ray got back to his adopted family's apartment and found that he was, once again, an orphan.

"The place was cleared out."

Ray saw nothing but mercy in their desertion, though.

"He didn't want me to get hurt," he whispered, sounding like a priest giving absolution.

But Ray still hurt.

He knew enough not to ask around about what happened.

Now, out on the street, the shopkeepers, the men in the Lexuses looked right through him. He was nobody again.

This time, though, Ray sounded relieved to be invisible.

"I figured I'd better get out of the hood fast," he said breathlessly as though he was still on the run, "until somethin' came up."

What finally came up was a desperate year on the streets and a string of bodega robberies.

"Crazy thing was I knew the people I was robbin'," Ray confessed. "Nice people. I swear they'd wait twenty minutes after I left before they called the cops. And they'd never really say it was me."

"But the drugs started getting me nuts again. Sick, paranoid, freezing cold even in July. That's when I got the idea I'd rob the Army and Navy store for some warm stuff. I thought I was pretty slick, walking out wearing three sweaters and two pairs of pants. But the cops were waiting for me outside."

Which brought Ray to that final point on his graph—a year's sentence, "a bullet" in the county jail, and his twenty-first birthday.

I noticed Ray hadn't put any mark down yet to signify this special birthday. Instead he stared at the paper and started calculating something on a piece of scrap.

"I figure in twenty-one years, I've only lived out in the world, you know, free, not locked up somewhere, for a total of six years and four months," he announced.

Then pointing toward my shirt pocket, Ray asked if he could use my paper-marking pen.

With a razor-thin red slash, he ended his life with this particular month, day, and year.

"I just hope God gets a light at the end of the tunnel for people like me," he pleaded.

"I don't wish nobody to have a life like mine. I don't wish that on *nobody.*"

He held the paper at arm's length.

It wasn't that white anymore. And there were holes where Ray had pressed hard as though trying to get through that tunnel he hoped God would light up the end of for him.

Ray put the paper down on the table. He pushed his chair back, stood up, and slowly started to walk along the edges of the cluttered classroom.

It wasn't his usual frantic pacing. Those days he'd roam the room, knocking into chairs and desks and the other guys.

"Yo, man, watch the fuck where you're going, will ya," Wilson or Dre or Boil would shout, guys who navigated Ray's craziness twenty-four hours a day.

"Come on, Ray, you know you can't go walking around," O'Shay, the classroom CO, would reason even though he knew it wouldn't do any good.

"The chair or the block," he'd end up threatening. "You decide."

But that day Ray's journey was different. Silent and deliberate, he walked as though he was moving back through his life to some happier time, or at least to one where there was less pain.

Watching him that morning reminded me of another procession.

When I was a kid in Catholic school, the nuns would march us across the playground every Friday afternoon during Lent to the parish church for the Stations of the Cross.

Once the sisters had corralled us squirming kids into the pews and glared us into silence, the priest would come from behind the altar and slowly walk around the church, counting out the final hours of another Man of Sorrows.

Even though we all knew the story by heart, and were happy to get out of Friday math, we always walked out of that church service pretty shaken up by the man's misery and remarkable bad luck.

That morning as Ray moved around the classroom I felt that same sadness.

But it didn't last long.

Ray came back to the table and grinned down at me.

I'd gotten it all wrong. It was Ray's twenty-first birthday and cause for celebration.

He sat down, hunched over the map of his life, and with a few strokes of my red pen ended it.

Then he pushed the paper toward me.

At first he scowled as I looked it over. He wasn't sure I was up to facing his life.

Finally, though, his eyes softened and he pulled his life out of my hands.

"It's all good," he declared as he lightly brushed his fingers across his bumpy lifeline.

"It's all good," he repeated, this time as though he wanted to comfort me.

It was a phrase that chorused through many of these young men's stories.

When I first heard it, it seemed like nothing more than bitter fruit: Nothing matters. Nobody cares. Nobody can touch me. It's all good.

For some it meant just that.

But for others, like Ray, I learned that it was more a reminder, a wisdom teaching: no matter how bad it gets, no matter how much pain there is, life *is* all good, *all* lives are good.

It wasn't sand castle optimism but rather bedrock belief. Maybe it was only a rock as small as Joey's lucky rock, but that reminded me that our hearts, those great guiding lodestones of love and life, are only as big as our fists.

Looking at the rugged plod of his life, I realized that Ray might've had a fist that he used too many times for his own good, but he also had a heart much bigger than his fist, a heart that could pull the good out of life.

I could see that it *was* all good for Ray.

After all, he had survived twenty-one years of this life. And hadn't a stranger, just the night before, given him a whole bag of Oreo cookies? Better yet, hadn't Ray had someone to share them with?

Down at the bottom of the paper I read his final flourish.

There, in red marker pen, he wished what I had heard him wish so often before for himself, his friends, his peoples, the world: PEACE! ONE LOVE!

Chapter Four

Pinups

Too much cleavage, not enough clothes.

The issue was pinups. The Department of Corrections called them pornography. The guys I taught called them "just some pictures of honeys."

It wasn't my battle. This one was between DOC and the hormone-crazed teenage boys the courts kept locking up.

But despite all the concrete walls and metal bars, everything spills into everything else in jail, and everyone's business is everyone else's business. Inevitably, the great debate spilled into my classroom.

The arguments were worthy of the Supreme Court.

Or so my students thought.

Angel, for example.

"But, Mr. C, what if my *mother* sent me them pictures. They can't call that porn," Angel said, and blushed.

Which he very well should have.

I knew his mother. She worked days in food services at the VA hospital, and at night and on weekends she was the pastor of a small storefront church in Peekskill, the Eternal Believers in Jesus. Twice a week she took a long ride across four towns on three buses to see her youngest offspring.

Besides, the mother argument didn't convince anyone, not even me, and I was usually a soft touch, something Warden Clooney would've loved to hear me admit.

But I'd heard enough stories about what mothers will do for their locked-up sons not to buy the argument. I knew about those mothers who laced balloons with cocaine, then hid them in their bras or up their sleeves and passed them to their boys when they hugged them for their once-a-visit embrace. All that was left was a quick swallow, then hours later those same sons hunched over their toilet bowls, rooting through their own shit looking for the balloon.

"They're only pictures of my girl, for chrissake," Angel went on, as though there was a case to be won and he'd get the photos back.

"*My girl.*

"I mean, it's not like I ain't seen it all before," he grumbled.

And now, of course, everybody else had "seen it all," too. Once corrections sliced open an envelope to check for contraband, what's in it that shouldn't be became county property.

Including butt-naked seventeen-year-old Natania.

At least Angel assumed it was her. Some of those photographs were so up close they looked like illustrations for a gynecological textbook. It was impossible to attach those body parts to any particular human being.

"She's my friggin' girl, and it's my friggin' business, nobody else's," Angel whined, not willing to let it go.

Of course, Angel didn't get it.

There wasn't much he did get. At seventeen he still couldn't read past a fourth-grade level and probably never would since he was limited in what he could do, and what effort he was willing to put into doing it.

Looking around the classroom, though, I could see by the snickers on the other kids' faces that they got it. I was surprised somebody hadn't shouted out what they all were thinking, "Yo, stupid, didcha ever stop to wonder who was takin' those beaver shots?"

But not all the guys were as ingenuous as Angel.

Playboy and *Penthouse* were contraband for minors. When they managed to get a copy, usually from the older guys who'd swap anything for food, they'd stash it in a dirty laundry bag or under their mattresses. Once the magazine had been pawed over—and everything else—by the boys on the block, they'd tear the pictures out and tape them to the inside of their sneakers or press them between the sheets of the toilet-paper roll they kept under their bunks, or stuff them down the hollow metal legs of a bunk bed.

Then after DOC did one of their periodic shakedowns and found the luscious babes, the guys would invent new hiding places, including the pages of one of my American history or literature textbooks. It didn't help my lesson much when one of those ladies wearing nothing but a straw hat and riding a motorcycle would fall on the floor as I flipped the book open.

Then again, maybe it did.

None of this hide-and-seek, search and destroy, stopped the dispute.

What about those broads in them weight-lifting magazines? Or those hot rod and truck magazines with the babes popping out of the sunroof wearing practically nothing but the car?

"What are they gonna say?" Freddy, who made his living chopping cars up for parts, would bluster with the injustice of it all. "Ya can't hang a picture of your favorite car on your locker door?"

Then there were the celebrity pics. Who needed *Playboy* when you could get a copy of *The Source* or *Vibe* or the swimsuit issue of *Sports Illustrated?*

And if you were really desperate you could cut out ads for bras and panties and thongs from the glossy Sunday circulars.

But most guys were happy just having pictures of their girl-friend's latest birthday party or shots of the last time they went to Jones Beach together.

Everybody that was but Wade.

Wade had his own set of pinups.

Although he had a few pictures taped to his locker door like most of his cell mates, he carried his pictures, a dozen or so photographs, rubber banded together in his pant pocket.

Wade was eighteen and facing serious state time. He had stabbed an eighteen-year-old in the eye in a movie theater in the Bronx. It was the final act in a long predator-prey series of events: a gunshot wound that shattered Wade's collarbone, three ribs of the other kid broken with a baseball bat, Wade's sister's apartment trashed and the bed set on fire, and then, that final evening with a knife in the Bronx theater.

Unfortunately for Wade, it suddenly became the business of the police, probably because it was the third stabbing in that theater in a month, and the manager had had it. So Wade and his deck of photos were on their way upstate.

I'd known Wade before he came to jail, when he was fifteen and going to the alternative high school where I taught just before coming to the jail. Even then, Wade wasn't like the other kids who'd been kicked out of their home schools and exiled to the alternative program. He didn't come to school to cause trouble. He didn't miss a day, and he didn't miss a class. I'd like to say that he didn't miss an assignment but that wasn't true. For Wade school was the one place he felt safe and loved.

And Wade *was* loved. The girls buzzed around him with his honey-colored skin and almond-shaped eyes that seemed to be blind to beauty. Short or tall, stubby or willowy, black or white, every girl swore that *she* was his special shorty and that's how he treated them. He walked them to class, he carried their books. When a girl talked to him, he looked into her eyes and really listened.

All that jealousy could have erupted in the parking lot but didn't. The girls knew better. Wade was a peacemaker, at least at school.

Maybe that was why he also got along with the other guys. He wasn't about territory. He'd as soon turn out his pockets for you, or jump up and give you his seat, than get into a stare-down match.

Which never happened.

Wade was an exotic.

He'd been places and done things the rest of the boys, even the older guys, couldn't imagine. They knew that no matter how hard they grunted over their weights in their families' finished basements they'd never be as diesel as Wade. He had a bulk and articulation you only got in places like Spofford Juvenile Detention or Woodfield Cottage. Although the girls thought the cut over his left eye and the healed gash across his jawbone was sexy, the boys knew what those scars were all about without even hearing the war stories that trailed him like an undercover cop.

It was back then, at the alternative program, that I first saw Wade's photographs.

He'd missed first period with me that day, the first time ever. I knew enough about his life to be concerned.

During my free period I looked around for someone from his bus. The only one I could find was Arlene. She was new to the school, and I'd seen Wade gallantly shepherding her through her first few weeks despite her pasty skin, pimples, and full braces. Which she brandished at me when I asked her if she knew where Wade was.

"No!" she snapped, so I knew something was up, but I'd have to wait to find out.

Right after lunch Wade came into my empty classroom. It was nothing more than four long tables a local church had donated to us when they had cleaned out their basement, the kind of tables women played bingo on. I often wondered if they had better luck than my students.

Wade pulled a chair up to the head of the table where I was correcting papers, what papers there were.

"Sorry I missed class this morning, Mr. C," he said.

"And I'm sorry Arlene was rude to you. She's, you know, just a kid and thinking she was covering for me."

"Well, she scared me off good enough." I laughed and waited.

Somehow I knew I wasn't about to get "the dog ate my alarm clock" excuse.

Whatever else Wade was, he was truthful. I also knew that he wouldn't bullshit me about making up the assignment he missed.

He'd say what he had to say when he was ready.

"I missed the bus this morning," he said, staring down, spinning a pen around on the table.

It was the first time I noticed that the top section of his baby finger was bent sideways away from the others, a break left untended.

Another chapter in this boy's story.

"I mean, I didn't really miss it. I was there at the stop," he went on.

"Arlene and me get on at the same corner. I had her books, you know, doing the big brother thing. We were just chillin'. I was gassing her up, trying to make her feel better because she was goin' on about how the other girls hate her.

"I think I really scared the shit out of her, though."

He looked up at me. "Sorry."

"Anyway, I saw these two dudes out of the corner of my eye, and I just dropped her books and ran through the backdoor of the Korean market where we wait." He sounded winded and stopped for a second.

"What was the problem with the two guys?" I asked to give him time to catch his breath.

"I'm their problem." He sighed as though he regretted the inconvenience.

"They're cousins with a Mount Vernon kid I got beef with. He shot one of my buddies behind the 7-Eleven in New Rochelle and so I got him back. I mean, he's still alive. I'm not that stupid. But these guys are after me now."

He studied me from underneath his thick black eyebrows.

"I ain't been anywhere all week, just keeping on the down low, figuring something else would happen.

"Well, this morning, it almost did.

"They had a gun and I wasn't expecting anything, because, I mean, man, I was on my way to school." Wade blew out his breath.

"Shit—sorry—they coulda killed Arlene. I just ran."

We both sat silently in our disbeliefs: Wade, that these guys would've dared shoot him on his way to school. I, that he bothered to thread his way through back streets and hitch rides to get there at all.

By then, the next period had started. I called my principal and told her I was with a student, and asked that someone cover my next class in what we called the library. It was just a storage room with boxes of used books from another church basement.

Wade slumped in his chair and finally seemed to relax. Maybe because he didn't have to go to class and pretend that everything was cool, no big deal. Or maybe because he finally realized he was safe—in school.

"Did I ever show you the pictures of my Moms, Mr. C?" Wade asked as he pulled out a deck of photos from his jacket pocket.

I didn't know much about Wade. I made some of the same guesses that the other students made about him from the little bits I heard.

I knew he was the second oldest in a family of five. He had a younger brother he was always yelling at over the phone in the guidance counselor's office because the kid wasn't going to school. I'd never heard of a father or a mother, nor a grandmother or aunt, nobody really. Wade seemed to be his own parent, and a parent to all the rest of his siblings.

But now he had photos to show of his mother.

Wade pulled his chair even closer to mine and laid his pictures out one at a time as though he were reading tarot cards.

"Isn't she beautiful?" He peered closely at the photo.

"Where was this taken?" I asked. "A costume party?"

The woman, who almost leaned out of the picture frame, looked no more than twenty. Her complexion was ebony, her face and shoulders broad. She wore a pink silk blouse with barely enough buttons to keep her full breasts in place. Cocked over one eye was a leather cowboy hat. It was hard to see Wade in her. But then the inscription settled all doubts: "To My Baby Wade, Love Mommy."

"No, man, she's goin' out clubbin'."

Wade clearly couldn't believe my stupidity.

I wanted to ask who was home taking care of his brothers

and sisters, but I held my tongue. Those pictures were clearly his talismans.

Slowly, one by one, he laid them out.

"This one's when she came home from the hospital after havin' Tanisha, my little sister. And this one's her pretending to play basketball with me and my buddies."

Pretend is right.

There was no way she could've moved very fast in those shorts, that tank top, and those heels.

"And this is her after her first week in detox." Wade pushed it toward me as proud as a new father.

"Mommy'd been shootin' up, right after Tanisha was born," Wade confided.

"Something got her real crazy. She'd be depressed, then she'd get real wild, out partyin' all night.

"One time she didn't come home for three days, and I hadda go looking for her. I found her in one of those crack houses over on Warbush Ave. I thought I'd have to kill the scum bucket who owned the place. He was acting like she *wanted* to stay there and not come home with me."

Wade didn't really have to tell me about the drugs. Even though she was scrubbed up in the photo, the picture all but gave off the sickly sweet smell of someone who'd lived in their own vomit for a while.

She was skeletal, hollowed eyed, and haunted looking.

The next batch were snapshots of Mommy at rehab working in the kitchen; Mommy in a group; Mommy folding laundry; Mommy holding Tanisha and Tucker, his youngest brother, on her lap; Mommy in her cowboy hat getting ready to go to her first clean and sober dance.

She never put back on all the pounds she lost. Her flesh had been permanently scraped from the bone. What she had gained was firmer and glowed more. But her eyes were still lost in her thin face; and they stared out at the camera as though puzzled about who this young boy was making such a fuss over her, and who this woman was who he was bothering with.

"And here she is." Wade proudly played his last card.

"This is her graduation from the program. Ninety days clean and sober."

She smiled out from a bouquet of daises, a bunch of balloons, and her framed diploma. She seemed as pleased with herself as her son was with her that day he showed me that final picture.

I didn't ask how long ago the snapshot had been taken or how his mother was doing. For that moment, in the quiet of the classroom, they both seemed eternally safe.

But it certainly hadn't worked out that way for Wade.

Soon after the gun incident at the bus stop, Wade disappeared, word was, down South.

But three or four years later, when he showed up in my jail classroom, I wasn't surprised, and I don't think he was surprised to see me. By then he didn't seem to have much wonder left in him.

But he was still a charmer.

He knew everybody. Inmates, COs, nurses, wardens.

Watching him walk down a hallway was like watching a politician work a suburban train station during campaign season, but with a lot more sincerity. Everybody had something for him, a smile, a wave, a joke, a word. He accepted each gesture as though that person was the only person in the world for the moment.

But the Wade who walked those halls was a lot more scarred and battered than the fifteen-year-old who I first got to know sitting at those luckless church tables.

I soon found out that things hadn't worked out any better for his mom.

It wasn't long after the pinup controversy started that I got to see Wade's stack of photos again. I knew he still carried them around. They stuck out of his baggy county oranges, outlined like a deck of forbidden playing cards.

He never took them out during school, and I never saw him

showing them to anyone. By then, probably everyone had seen them plenty of times. It wasn't until Angel had had Natania's pictures confiscated that they appeared from Wade's pocket.

The writing assignment I'd put on the board clearly couldn't match the interest I saw in their eyes as Wade and Angel huddled together at the table's end.

One by one Wade laid out his photos. Angel carefully fingered each picture, and Wade whispered in his ear. They were so intent, so mesmerized, that I began to wonder if maybe Wade had played a card trick of his own and switched what I assumed were his mommy pictures for ones with a lot more fascination.

I needn't have worried. Before I could casually snake my way across the room, one student at a time, to where they were sitting Wade called me over.

"Hey, Mr. C, I wanna show you my new pictures."

Angel quickly got up to give me his seat.

"I think I'll give the assignment a shot," he said, giving me a shot with his shy smile. "Yo, dawg, thanks for settin' me straight and showin' me your pictures of your Moms."

"Keep it real, bro," Wade said as he disengaged himself from their intricate tangle of finger snaps and hugs, and sat down across from me.

Suddenly, that same breathless fifteen-year-old of years ago was sitting in front of me again. Did he remember spinning a pen on the table just that way that morning in that other classroom?

"I only hit her that once," he quietly exploded, as though he'd been holding it back all those years, as though I'd silently accused him of something I knew nothing about.

"Mommy kept doin' these programs, ninety days, ninety days, ninety days, but she just couldn't stay away from the crack. After a while the judge got sick of her and just locked her up, said forget about the detox stuff, and put her in jail.

"Me and my Aunt Brenda kept the kids together. Well, my aunt really, I was running around with my own shit.

"But this one time, though, I was home after doin' six months here in this joint, tryin' to stay clean and off the streets, and she was really fucked up, all the time, couldn't even get outta the house for the shit.

"So these slime bags brought it to her. One actually handed it to my little sister. My little sister!

"That's when I hit her. I came home, and there were these needles all over the place, and my brother and sisters and my little cousins running around. I went nuts and smacked her. I had to. She was killin' herself, and those babies.

"Aunt Brenda had to pull me off her.

"But then Mommy called the cops on me. I got out before they came. That's when they finally brought her to the hospital, so at least somethin' good came out of it."

Wade finally looked up.

"But we're cool now though." He smiled, assuring both of us.

"Want to see my pictures?" he begged.

The woman who stared out from those pictures barely resembled the mommy he proudly showed off four years ago.

But Wade didn't seem to notice. He was just as proud and pleased with the woman who was almost lost in the pillows and sheets of her hospital bed as he had been of her in her leather cowboy hat. Her once polished ebony complexion was now ashen, and what little flesh she had was taut on sharp bone as though she had become the needle that killed her.

Wade didn't bother with a diagnosis. He knew he didn't have to. So many of his friends had already lost mothers and fathers to AIDS. Instead he celebrated her life for what it was right then.

There he sits on her bed, Mommy propped up with pillows, his arm around her angled shoulders, smiling for the camera. In another picture, Wade stands, a floating head, behind a monitor of some kind, his mother's face, a worn profile on an ancient coin, turned quizzically to the side as though searching for him. Wade pushes her in a wheelchair down a narrow hospital corridor, then

Mommy hugs that same corridor wall, trailing an IV pole beside her, waving a hand at the camera as though to shoo him away, her smile shy but still flirtatious.

"And this is Mommy with the two Jamaican aides that took care of her most of the time," Wade said, placing the last photo on top of the others.

"That one there is Fatima, she was always yellin' at me for gettin' in the way." Wade laughed.

"But she loved me. She told Mommy I reminded her of her son back on the island. 'No good rascal he is, jus' like this one here.'

"And that's Harriet, on the other side of the bed.

"'She love da comera, mon.'" He mimicked her island lilt. "She's the one who took the pictures of us together."

There wasn't time to ask what happened to Mommy. The 2:15 bell had already sounded for mandatory lockdown for the 2:30 shift change. Wade should've been on his way back to his block minutes ago.

"I gotta go, Mr. C," Wade said as he scooped up his pictures, put the blue rubber band around them, and slipped them back into his oranges.

"I promise to get to that essay first thing tomorrow morning," he shouted as he disappeared through the door.

I could hear him as he trotted down the hallway toward his block. He was late, but I knew he wouldn't get written up. What CO would slap a discipline report on a kid who was the only one, all day, who noticed that you got a haircut, or who told you he appreciated you giving him a little extra time with the teacher?

Not long after that, Wade disappeared again, this time to begin his five-year bid in state prison.

Since then I've often wondered what pictures he had to show up there. Even if he survived his first year, (and each scar on his face placed the odds against him making it), his mother certainly wouldn't. She'd be dead years before he got out.

Then what calling cards would he use?

I hadn't asked Wade about his younger brothers and sisters, whether they were born infected with HIV. But no matter what their health, I could easily imagine him with a deck of new photos spread out on a mess hall table for a bunch of upstate inmates.

"This one here, this picture? That's my sister Tanisha going to school. And see those shoes, I helped pay for those shoes. Well, at least a little bit.

"And here's my little man Tucker on his bike."

But I wasn't so easy about how well Wade's style of pinups would go down in state prison.

I'd heard enough grizzled, older guys, prison veterans who'd done hard time, warn the younger ones.

"You all think you're such hot shit. But I'm tellin' ya. What plays here ain't necessarily gonna play upstate."

Boobs, butt, and beaver?

No problem.

But home and heart?

I worried that for some people, themselves mired in the state prison system for years, Wade's brand of intimacy might cut too close to the bone. I worried that some upstate inmate, or CO, or even some burned-out, bitter warden might feel this punk had hit too close to home. And I worried that one of them might just decide somebody should do something about that.

Chapter Five

Ghost Story

M r. C! Mr. C!" Luis called out, waving and smiling, as he made his way toward me down the hall.

I was used to this kind of encounter.

Old students discharged a month, six months, even a few years ago, would show up back on the jail census.

Eventually we'd run into each other and they'd greet me with wide smiles as though they were back for homecoming weekend at their old school and had spotted me, a beloved old teacher, walking across the campus quad.

I knew where those welcoming smiles came from. For many of the guys the jailhouse classroom was one of the few places where someone had been nice to them and cared about them.

Still, I would pin them with a disapproving stare.

"Hey, this isn't a summer camp, you know, where you come back every year," I'd growl. "I'm not happy to see you. What are you doing locked up again?"

I had been teaching in my new jail classroom for a few years when I first met Luis. He was one of those inmates who, in an odd twist of logic, flourished behind bars. He never got any write-ups, was always polite to correctional staff and the other men, and was constantly brokering the peace among the younger guys who usually were quick to take offense.

When he was discharged this last time a little over a year ago, I was hopeful he wouldn't be back. Since he had been sentenced to a full county bid of eight months, he had had time to study for his GED and get some drug counseling.

My optimism was helped by the fact that Luis wasn't like many of the other men who blamed their incarceration on "the system," or "the white man," or "the gov'ment."

You didn't hear him claiming that he "caught a charge," as though misdemeanors and felonies were predatory viruses floating around infecting the innocent and unsuspecting. He seemed to understand the world that was created for him, and the world he created for him.

So when he insisted he was ready to put jail and the streets behind him, I believed him.

But here he was again.

"Luis," I said, our hands grasping, sliding, fingers snapping against each other in the latest jailhouse shake.

"Yo, Mr. C, gangsta! You got that down pretty good," Luis teased.

"Not bad for an old white man, hey?" I loved embarrassing these guys, saying what I knew they were thinking.

"But seriously, I'm disappointed to see you again."

Suddenly, his smile vanished.

"They kilt him, Mr. C," Luis whispered. "They kilt my brother."

He hunched toward me, as though "they" might overhear.

It was a possibility in this place.

All the guys were opened to constant threats and assaults from all directions. It might be their victim's friends or their family, rival gang members, or their codefendants they turned state's evidence against.

Some of the younger kids put themselves on PC status, protective custody. That way they were housed on a separate unit and only moved through the halls under the protection of an officer.

But most inmates didn't want that protection. PC was "soft."

And of course you certainly never reported any threat or incident to DOC, since to "rat someone out" was one of the grimiest offenses you could commit. If you did, everybody agreed you deserved to get the shit beaten out of you.

In the system the only honorable way to protect yourself was to watch your back, and your peoples' backs.

"You remember my baby brother, Felipe." Luis barely got the words out.

"Of course I remember him." I nodded.

Felipe was just a little boy when I encountered him in the county lockup. He was barely fifteen years old, small for his age. His smooth, hairless skin, fine cheekbones, and matchstick limbs made him look about ten.

But he had the mouth and the spunk of a seasoned jailbird. He was always coming into class (that is when he wasn't on lockdown for some fight or belligerence to staff) with a busted lip or a black and yellow eye swollen shut.

Luis, on the other hand, was tall, big boned, with wide shoulders and paddle hands. He had the same chiseled features of his little brother, but unlike Felipe, whose complexion was pale white, Luis's was polished hazelnut.

Although they both had the same straight black hair they got from their Taino mother, Luis's was sheared close while Felipe's was a mad mop. That difference in hairstyles said a lot about their personalities. Luis was restrained, soft-spoken, and deliberate. His brother was fiery, loudmouthed, and brash.

I had Luis and Felipe in different classes, a separation that had more to do with abilities than age.

Luis was preparing for his GED. Although he was eligible to take the test in Spanish, he was determined to do it in English.

On the other hand, Felipe was struggling to learn to read—to read in anything, Spanish or English. He was barely literate in either.

I never could figure out if Felipe just couldn't learn, or if he just couldn't give school the attention it needed. He seemed hardwired for vigilance and distraction.

In class his head was constantly swiveling around, jerking up at the slightest sound. It was impossible for his eyes to settle on the page.

But even when he was alone, Felipe's world was one of constant threat.

One day he came to class with his pant legs tucked into his white socks. When I jokingly made a motion to tug them out, saying, "Hey, Felipe, what's with this?" he pushed my hand away, then quickly apologized.

"That's to keep the ghosts out," he told me, pulling me into a quiet corner of the room.

"The other night my grandpa came into my cell and sat on my bed. But I wouldn't talk to him.

"Later when I told Mamita, she said it was the ghosts trying to get back at me because I hadn't listened to abuelito when he told me to stay inside the night I got arrested. That was the same night he died. So she told me I should put an apple over my cell door to keep him away.

"But you know me, Mr. C"—he sucked his teeth and shook his head in this knowing way he had, like an old man talking about his faraway recalcitrant youth—"I don't listen to her, I don't listen to nobody, and now the ghosts are trying to sneak inside me, so I do this to ward them off."

Luis had heard about what happened from Manny, another student in the class. Manny was a Jamaican with a full rigging of dreadlocks tied behind his back. He was constantly haggling for food.

"Hey, mon, I give you two girlie magazines for some jerky, the spicy kind," he'd barter right in class, right there in front of me.

Luis didn't have any problem figuring out what kind of currency to use with Manny. He'd supply him with hot sauce, beans, and dried chilies if Manny kept a protective eye on his baby brother.

"Manny told me what happened, Mr. C," Luis said, having weaseled his way into my classroom just minutes before the mandatory lockdown for the 2:30 shift change.

"Our mother's big into Santeria," he explained somewhat embarrassedly, "and ever since we was kids she says she sees all these ghosts swirling around us.

"Poor Felipe's been really scared of them all his whole life."

Whatever those forces were, they'd kept Felipe combative and suspicious. The last time he was discharged I knew I'd see him again.

But I was wrong.

Luis came back in his place.

"The Armenians, they kilt him," he murmured, his head down, afraid someone might read his lips.

"They shot him dead," he said, his big eyes clouded with tears, the lashes so black they seemed outlined with mascara.

He moved closer to the concrete wall, looking away from a group of inmates walking by on their way to attorney visits.

"Luis, I'm really sorry," I said.

He pushed himself away from the wall and glanced around trying to seem disinterested.

"Yeah, well, thanks, Mr. C," he answered, clearly anxious to move on. We both knew that tears in jail were a guaranteed invitation to harassment.

"How about you come into the classroom for a couple of minutes?" I suggested. "Class doesn't start for a while. That way we can talk."

"Yeah, yeah, that'd be cool." He looked up at me gratefully.

Once we got into my room, he sat with his back to the hallway window and slumped over the desk. He didn't say anything. He just shook his head every once in a while as though there was some part of a conversation he didn't understand. Then he'd get up for a Kleenex to blow his nose until finally I put the box of tissues on the chair next to him, out of sight of the hallway.

"You know, Mr. C, I keep thinking, if I'd only gotten there five minutes sooner he'd still be alive. Five minutes," Luis said over and over, as though if he repeated it enough times, the words would bring Felipe back.

"A stupid haircut." Luis shook his head in disbelief.

"We was meeting in the Bronx. Felipe wouldn't let anybody else cut his hair except this guy, Bernardo.

"You remember his hair! Well, my mother begged me to make sure he got it cut for our grandmother's birthday. Abuelita was going to be seventy.

"That was the day they kilt him, on her birthday."

Luis was late because he had been running errands for his mother.

"You know my mother, she can't get around that easy, so I was getting stuff for the party, down on Arthur Ave."

I had met Luis's and Felipe's mother at the jail's parents' night.

She was wheelchair bound, a speck of a woman almost lost in a swath of blankets and scarves. She arrived with quite the entourage. Luis's younger sisters hovered around her, tucking in all her raiment in a solemn parody of the age-old bedtime ritual while Luis's aunt Ramona, his mother's older sister, was in charge of pushing her.

But all their ministrations stopped once Luis got there. As soon as they saw him, they stepped back like courtiers in court and watched his approach. When his mother saw him weaving his way around the other visitors, her face broke out of its usual worried scowl into a big smile.

Luis knelt down in front of her, grabbed her hands, and started to chatter to her, their foreheads almost touching.

"I had all the stuff in my car, the roasting pig—Abuelita loves her pig—the vegetables. My man Freddy packed it all in ice for me because he knew we was going to meet Felipe first before we went home." Luis smiled, then remembered.

"As soon as we pulled up to the curb I knew something was wrong." He looked out across the room. "There was a whole bunch of people out front of Bernardo's.

"At first I figured somebody was getting the shit beat outta him, somebody's always got beef with somebody else in the Bronx, usually about some girl who's not worth looking at.

"But then I see this kid, Dante, I know, running across the street to the bodega and shouting something.

"By then I was worried about Felipe. He was always getting into fights, and the last thing he needed was to get another probation violation.

"So I shoved my way to the front of the crowd, and there he was on the ground, his man Paco with his shirt off stuffing it into Felipe's stomach with all this blood gushing out.

"When Paco saw me, he started yelling at me to get out, the Armenians were looking for me, too. I didn't know what the hell he was talking about. Armenians? But by then I was screaming for somebody to call the EMTs and I knelt down and laid his head in my lap telling him, 'Hang on, baby brother, hang on.'"

Luis was there now.

"Mr. C, I don't know if he could even hear me, his eyes kept moving like he was trying to open them, but he didn't have the strength.

"By then I'd taken the shirt from Paco and was pressing with all my might, trying to force the blood from coming out, but he just kept getting paler and paler and the shirt got redder and redder."

The more Luis talked, the more the dark hues of his own brown skin drained from his face, as though it was his blood that was seeping out from the four bullet wounds Felipe took in the stomach.

"He just died," Luis barely whispered.

Out in the hallway, carts with empty breakfast trays rattled by and inmates started moving back and forth to the barber, to sick call, to visits.

I'd asked the morning relief officer, CO Chase, to hold my students back on the blocks for a while. He was usually intractable when it came to DOC's procedures. But death is the universal leveler, especially in jail, where everyone, correctional staff and inmates alike, has suffered at least one heartbreaking loss. Chase knew Luis, and liked him as much as he liked anybody.

"I worked with that young fool, Felipe," he grumbled. "Didn't surprise me when I heard.

"I'll hold your guys back fifteen minutes, Mr. C, but that's it, no more."

It was already a half hour.

Luis stared down at the table, the way I imagined he did holding his dying brother, staring intently at Felipe's eyes willing them to open.

But he was dry-eyed because he knew there were dozens of eyes in that Bronx crowd storing up those tragic but familiar images so they could gossip them back to their friends and report them to his enemies.

And he was equally dry-eyed, I was sure, when the cops finally arrived on the scene.

"I kept telling the cops I didn't know nothing about any Armenians." He looked up at me suddenly angry. "I mean, up until then I didn't even know what an Armenian was. So how could they want to kill me or my baby brother?"

But Luis knew the anonymous gangs that rivaled on the streets; and he knew Felipe wasn't always the little brother he used to take on camel rides at the Bronx Zoo. His mother had always worried about the evil ghosts getting her baby boy. Luis, in his own way, had, too.

"They kilt my brother, and they almost kilt Mamita," he went on.

"We had to put her in the hospital. Abuelita stayed with her the whole time. The only time she left was for the funeral.

"But little by little she got stronger, and when she finally came home she was real calm.

"I carried her up the stairs that first day, and after I put her on the couch, she made me go around the house and put all the pictures we had of Felipe facedown.

"She told me that the spirits had talked to her while she was in the hospital and said that Felipe was with the Virgin, and that she shouldn't worry, but to be careful because the same evil ghosts that got Felipe were trying to get to me and my little sisters.

"I got scared, Mr. C, real scared," he said, looking up at me for the first time, his eyes wide with leftover fear. "I mean, not about the ghosts, but because I thought maybe Mamita was going crazy."

But it turned out his mother had a plan.

She made Luis promise that he and his friends wouldn't seek revenge. She made him swear on his brother's grave that nobody would die because of what happened.

"She said we had to be done with all the killing because all she kept seeing while she was in the hospital was blood, blood all over the walls and on the sheets and on people's hands, and that if I ended up getting kilt, too, she'd die.

"Of course I promised and I really meant it." Luis sat up straight with the memory of his resolve.

"But then she really blew me away." He smiled.

"She said we was all going to move, the whole family, me and my sisters, Abuelita, Auntie Ramona, and her two boys. We was going to go and live in New Haven. You know, in Connecticut?"

And they did.

Auntie Ramona's boyfriend had cousins who lived in New Haven. They helped them find a big house, schools for the younger children, and a job for Luis working in a Jiffy Lube.

"I never thought Mamita would ever smile again after losing Felipe," he confessed. "But once we got up there and she saw that things could be different from the way they was in Yonkers, she didn't cry so much or worry every time one of us left the house."

But eventually Felipe's ghostly nemesis moved up to Connecticut as well.

"One day my little sister Amanda came home and told me that these white guys stopped her on the street and said that they were friends of Felipe's and they wanted to know where I was working." Luis leaned closer as he talked and started looking over his shoulder again.

"She's a smart kid and didn't say anything to them. And she didn't say anything to Mamita about it, either.

"I went nuts.

"I didn't know who these guys were, I mean, I knew they were the same Armenians who shot Felipe, but I still didn't know why they kilt him, or why they were after me.

"But I knew that I couldn't let nothing happen to my sisters. Christ, for all I knew they'd go for Auntie or even Abuelita.

"That's when I got the gun.

"At first I didn't tell nobody, but everybody knew something was going on with me 'cause I was edgy all the time and started screaming at my sisters and little cousins, even Mamita," he said, even now regretting his outbursts.

"Finally, Auntie's boyfriend, Carlos, told me that he had heard that some New York guys were asking around about me and had I heard about it. I told him yeah and that I had a gun.

"After that was when everything started to happen.

"A bunch of my Yonkers friends, Ricardo, Freddy, and a couple of his cousins, all showed up in New Haven. Word was out in New York, they said, that this Armenian gang called the Hammers was out to get me, and they figured I needed some backup.

"By then I didn't know what I needed. Mamita had to go to the emergency room one time after I yelled at her, and then Abuelita started screaming at me, saying I was killing my own mother.

"That's why, once Freddy and them showed up, I decided I had to get out of New Haven, away from Mamita and do something.

"Luckily, we didn't get stopped going on I-95, since Freddy told me later that they had a couple of semis stashed in the trunk."

Luis stopped, stared at his hands twisting around each other, then looked me straight in the eye.

"Mr. C, I didn't want any of this. I just wanted Mamita and Auntie and Abuelita and all of us to be safe and happy for once.

"I don't know what I was planning to do. I mean, I didn't even know what these Hammer guys looked like, but I kept driving around, showing myself, showing my guns, just wanting to get the whole thing over.

"I kept thinking no matter what happened to me, I was already dead. Part of me was dead with Felipe, and then if something happened to Mamita, that would kill the rest of me, so I had no choice.

"I knew the po-lice had been watching me, but by then I didn't care.

"When they finally pulled me over and started searching the car I didn't even bother to run. I just started to cry. I cried like I didn't cry when I was holding Felipe or when they put him in the ground.

"The cops found a couple of guns under my seat and one on me.

"They knew about Felipe. The Yonkers cops know everything. They even apologized when they cuffed me and put me in the squad car."

Luis slid down in the chair as though he was exhausted from the months of the chase and uncertainty, from all the crying.

But even now he knew he couldn't rest.

Because of his felony record he was looking at some serious time in state prison where he knew he'd never be safe. He'd never be able to stop looking over his shoulder. He'd never be sure whom he could trust; inmate or correctional staff, it didn't matter. His life would be haunted by the same dark ghosts that hunted Felipe down, those same phantom Armenians who themselves could never rest until their work was done and Luis was dead.

"You know, Mr. C, I use to make fun of Mamita and her spirits. But now I keep thinking that she was right, about, you know, the ghosts coming after us." Luis sighed, sitting up.

"She just didn't know what to call them, that's all. She didn't know Crips, or Bloods, or Netas, or Hammers.

"But it don't matter what you call them, 'cause they get you anyways, no matter how far away you run and what you do to start over. I know they'll get me, the way they got my baby brother. The only difference is, they got him a lot sooner."

Chapter Six

Shit-Eating Grin

Darquel stood in the doorway grinning.

A shit-eating grin.

That's what O'Shay, the classroom officer, called it.

Usually if some inmate came to class with a smirk like that, a big, cheesy, self-satisfied smile, O'Shay would have him spread-eagle against the wall, pat him down, underarms, chest, back, crotch, butt, legs, ankles, the whole nine.

"Some wise-ass punk comes in here looking like that, I know he's up to no good," he told me after class the first time it happened.

"Probably sneaking some weed to his homie, or he's got a shank down his pants, ready to cut some asshole who dissed him. Trust me, I know about this stuff."

If O'Shay didn't find anything on the guy, he'd tell him to wipe that shit-eating grin off his face or he'd wipe it off for him.

But this time O'Shay didn't do any of that.

Instead, he just nodded Darquel into the room, scowled up into his baby-cheeked face, and stared him in the eyes, that is, as much of his eyes as he could see since Darquel's long-lashed lids drooped over his black eyes.

"I don't take no crap from nobody, so sit down and do what the teacher tells you," he growled in his Bronx brogue at the still smiling seventeen-year-old.

"You do what you're supposed to do, mind your own business, and you'll be okay."

By then O'Shay had turned away from that goofy look and

glared down at the other students who sat ranked along the long table we used as a desk.

The guys didn't catch O'Shay's look, though. They were too busy gaping at Darquel. They were waiting to see what this new kid was going to do.

O'Shay had warned them about him a few days before he showed up at the door.

"Listen up, you hoodlums!" he barked out before sending them back to the block for chow.

"There's gonna be this new kid comin' to class from the forensic unit. He's kinda weird..."

"Well, he is," O'Shay interrupted himself, seeing the look on my face.

"Anyways, he's got this thing, he smiles all the time and laughs for no reason. But the docs think he's okay enough to be comin' to class, so we'll see.

"All I want is for you guys to leave him alone, make nicey-nice. Or at least pretend."

O'Shay was a big, burly Irishman who always sounded as though you were in deep-shit trouble, until that is, you really were, when you knew the difference. He didn't know how to talk any other way. Maybe it was his early years on the tough streets of Limerick and later on the equally tough streets of the Bronx.

Certainly his fifteen years working with the minors hadn't softened him up. It was a post that burned out even the toughest COs after a few years.

"You just gotta know your poison in a place like this if you wanna make it to retirement," he chortled when I asked him about his longevity there.

"Besides, with the minors you can kick butt all you want and get away with it."

Of course, O'Shay never said anything about the skinny-assed white kids he'd shepherded over the years through the jail's predator-prey food chain. Or the guys he saved from being taken down

by the goon squad, the young kids he claimed weren't really troublemakers just dumber than dirt. Or the smart ones he hooked up
with trusty jobs, real jobs on the repair crews that used their brains
as well as their muscle and tired them out so that they fell dead into
bed at night instead of joining the general midnight rabble.

"The first one of youse to make fun of this new kid? You're
dead, outta here. Not only that, you'll have my foot so far up your
butt, your tongue will be shoe leather," he finished up, spitting out
rags of tobacco from the black cigar stub he gnawed day in and day
out.

After they'd checked Darquel out, the other guys suddenly got
busy with their schoolwork. They shifted papers around or found
their place in their books. They spread out arms and legs and work-
sheets to fill up the space around them. Although they didn't dare
say it, nobody wanted Darquel sitting next to them.

Eventually O'Shay got him settled at the table.

After that they ignored him.

But he was hard to ignore.

His head was big and round as a pumpkin, and it didn't quite
set right on his broad shoulders, so that it bobbed from side to side.
Just looking at him, you felt your own balance threatened, and you
wondered how he stayed steady on his feet.

But that's not what really got your attention.

It was that smile.

It didn't matter what was going on, he grinned, he smirked, he
giggled, and every once in a while he gave a loud belly laugh about
nothing at all—as far as the rest of us could figure out.

I was a little more prepared for Darquel than the kids in my
class. I'd gotten the word on him from Dr. Abraham, the director
of the forensic unit's mental health block.

"The young man's on huge doses of medication," he explained
to me.

"Drugs to control everything from his asthma to his nervous
tics to his seizures to his voices."

Corrections was a tough place to work for someone in the mental health field. Nobody lasted long. Some nurses and psychiatrists couldn't see beyond the daily abuse they had to take from the inmates and correctional staff.

Others struggled with issues of confidentiality and mandated disclosure. They were reluctant to write things down, afraid that reports would get into the wrong hands.

Nurses and psychiatrists came and went as the flood tides of DOC bureaucracy and mistreatment swamped them. The good ones left quickly. The bad ones left, too; they just took a little longer.

But Dr. Abraham was one of the good ones, and he stayed through it all.

He was a bright, hard-working psychiatrist. Most of his colleagues had retired, or were at best consulting for huge fees. Although he came to the county lockup from a prestigious New York City teaching hospital, he was just as comfortable with the jail's squalor, as he no doubt had been with the sterile, orderly wards he walked, lecturing residents and interns.

I would see him all over the jail in his same brown tie and same brown tweed sports jacket, his reading glasses around his neck and the skullcap his wife knitted him balanced on his balding head.

He talked to whomever wanted to talk to him, wherever they felt most comfortable. He'd stand listening to a warden or a nurse or a maintenance worker as well as the inmates, the boys and men who were desperate for the stability and compassion he offered them, in the hallways or on the block.

"Darquel's going to have all those things—the voices, the inappropriate smile, the seizures—for the rest of his life, I'm afraid," Dr. Abraham explained.

"The guy's been through a lot in his sixteen, seventeen years.

"His mother was an addict when he was born. She died soon after, an overdose of pills and booze.

"We're not too sure what exactly happened to him after that. The records on this kid are pretty sketchy, he's been moved around so much. When he was five, for example, as far as I can figure out, he'd been moved nine times from relative to relative.

"And there's been all kinds of abuse. His seizure disorder probably comes from an uncle who used to tie him down to a radiator and...well, you don't need to know all that. If you're like me, it just makes you want to do things to the adults in these kids' lives that you didn't think you were capable of.

"Anyways, Darquel's definitely been sexually abused, and now he's gotten himself in trouble with a little girl in his neighborhood. So sexual issues are coming up a lot for him.

"His voices don't help. You should know that they're pretty explicit, and insistent. That's what the smiling and giggling is about, and from what he's told me there's nothing funny about them.

"We've been working with the voices. I'm trying to get him to think of them like having a radio on in the background. He just has to ignore them. Easier said than done, I know." Dr. Abraham sighed and shook his head.

"But he's a good kid," he rallied. "I want to give him a chance to get back into things, normal things, you know, like going to school."

"Well, I hope it works out for him," I hesitated.

I wasn't so worried about Darquel. It was more the other guys and their reactions to him that had me concerned.

But Dr. Abraham knew what I was talking about.

"I have no doubt O'Shay will take care of the other guys." He chuckled.

"I do suggest that you as the teacher set down clear rules for Darquel right from the start."

"And then, of course, get ready to ignore some pretty bizarre behavior." He smiled, holding on to his yarmulke as though heading down on the roller-coaster rails.

That first day, just before the class ended, I asked Darquel to stay for a minute after everybody else left. I wasn't sure he heard me. I wasn't even sure he knew I was there. But he stayed at the table when O'Shay herded the other guys out.

"Thanks for staying, Darquel," I said.

"Like he's got a goddamn choice," O'Shay snorted quietly, standing at the door behind me.

Darquel didn't answer. He just stared across the room away from O'Shay and me and twirled a hank of black nappy hair around a finger. He looked like a toddler—a very tall, stocky toddler—just waking up from his afternoon nap.

"I like to talk to all the new students, give them an idea of the class, tell them what I expect of them, that kind of thing."

Darquel grabbed another fingerful of hair in the other hand and twirled.

This time he gave the table a crooked smile.

"If you noticed, everybody has their own assignments to do. So, what I want to do is if you need help with the work, ask me, *not* the other students. That way nobody disturbs anybody else." I pushed ahead.

"There's no talking or fooling around.

"You need to stay in your seat.

"But if you ever feel like you need to go back to the block for any reason, that's okay, just let Officer O'Shay and me know.

"Is that clear?" I paused.

"Any questions?"

Darquel's fingers twirled even faster, and his grin got even broader.

I didn't hold out for an answer.

"I'll see you tomorrow."

I started to smile but stopped myself. I didn't know what territory that would lead me into.

It turned out that Darquel had a lot of tomorrows.

He didn't miss a day. He was there early, and he stayed the full time. He got work done even though he smiled and grinned and grimaced and giggled and mumbled to himself, and shifted his eyes from side to side at the students who ended up next to him.

But it was never the same student twice. The guys rotated

around the table away from him. It got to be a sort of lottery. They started getting to class earlier and earlier so they had a choice of seat away from him; and traffic in and out of the room for the bathroom slowed down considerably. They knew that if they left their space to pee they'd come back two seats down, their work folder right next to Darquel.

By the end of the first week, everybody accepted that Darquel wasn't going away. There hadn't been the circus or fireworks they'd expected, or hoped for, and they realized that they could only roll their eyes so many times or suck their teeth about this weirdo sitting there grinning, laughing, wheezing before they got bored.

A few times, one or two of the other students even asked Darquel to pass down some more paper or asked him if they could use one of the two erasers that floated around the room when he was finished.

Darquel didn't look up, but he did pass whatever was needed.

And once when Midnight, a short, husky twenty-year-old from the Dominican Republic, forgot himself and thanked him for letting him use the eraser, Darquel answered back in a shy voice, "You're welcome."

The days were quiet, as quiet as it gets in a jail classroom, until Puma got the note.

"I'm not takin' this shit, Mr. C," Puma sputtered.

He shoved the tattered corner of a paper toward me and scrubbed his hands against the top of his shirt.

"I'm sorry, but I'm not putting up with this. The guy's a fuckin' nutcase."

After I read what I could decipher of the note—the scrawl was childlike and filled with misspellings—I knew it was a waste of time to tell Puma to take it easy.

"Where was the note?" I asked

"I seen him stick it in my folder toward the end of class," Puma could barely get out.

I was lucky he hadn't found the note at the beginning of class.

I was luckier still that he hadn't jumped over the table and beaten the shit out of Darquel.

Try telling an adolescent boy, locked up for eight months, hormones sparking every nerve ending in his body so that just saying the word *girl* or *woman* or *shorty* or *bitch* sent his hand into his pants, that the note Darquel wrote, the note that said "I want to suck your hairy dick," had nothing to do with him.

Try telling him that it had nothing to do with sex or desire or wanting. It had to do with a confusion so powerful, so pressing, that it could conjure up voices in somebody like Darquel's head, voices that told him, commanded him to do things he didn't want to do, voices that told him the only way to get the love and attention and approval he never had when he was little was to obey them. That was why he smiled and smirked and snickered. He hoped that those things would placate those demanding demons, shut them up, or at least quiet them down enough so that they *were* just like a radio playing in the background the way Dr. Abraham said they were.

Try telling an adolescent boy battling his own relentless urges that this kid did all those things even though he knew the voices wouldn't leave him alone until he finally wrote a note like the one he slipped into Puma's papers.

Try telling a correctional officer the same things, and you'd get about as far as I would've gotten with Puma or any of my other students.

"You did the right thing, Puma," I said. "I really appreciate that you didn't flip out in class."

"Yeah, well, nothing better happen, 'cause my peoples are all over this place, even in forensic," he spit out, letting the threat hang in the air.

"Nothing is going to happen," I said firmly, not really sure that it wouldn't.

"Well, ain't that some shit," O'Shay said after sending Puma back to his block. He looked at me and waited.

I wasn't used to a silent O'Shay.

"I'm going to go and talk to Dr. Abraham," I said.

"Yeah, good to let them know on forensic. That way they can keep an eye out."

O'Shay hesitated.

"I'd hate to see anything happen to the kid." O'Shay cleared his throat, then got ahold of himself. "Well, to anybody."

When Dr. Abraham heard, he sighed.

"Ah, jeez, I'm sorry this happened. We've been adjusting his meds, trying to cut them back, but maybe it was too much, too soon. I'm really sorry," he apologized as though he was the one who had written the note.

"Well, actually, aside from this, things have been going pretty well for Darquel," I tried to reassure both of us.

"I mean, the other day a couple of the guys were actually joking around with him, calling him DQ, and for once he had a smile that seemed more pleased than his usual out-there grin.

"But what I need to know from you is where do I go with this?"

"Well, you definitely have to confront him about it.

"Read him the riot act. Tell him you *know* he wrote the note. I doubt he'll deny it. If he did it might actually be a sign of health… But, sorry, that's not helpful to you.

"Tell him that that kind of thing won't be tolerated. He knows what inappropriate means. He's been in enough psych hospitals," he said, sounding sterner than I'd ever heard him.

"Let him know that if it happens again, he doesn't come to school. I know school's important to him. He actually told me the other day that he liked it.

"Maybe that's why the voices made him write that note…." His own voice trailed off.

I didn't tell O'Shay about Dr. Abraham's speculations about why he might have written the note. He had a hard enough time with what he called my loosey-goosey liberalism. But he liked the part about the riot act.

"You know me, I like reaming ass," he joked, back in his element.

He called forensic to have Darquel escorted to class early.

Darquel and I sat across from each other at the table in the empty classroom while O'Shay stood less than a foot behind him.

He had insisted on that.

"Look, you never know with these guys," he bit off his words, working hard to sound reasonable.

"Don't forget where you are, for chrissake. They're not here on goddamn scholarship. Especially this one."

In the end I agreed.

O'Shay was right.

You never knew in jail.

Darquel wasn't any different during my talk than he was in class. He didn't look up, and his smile didn't dim. Instead of twirling his hair he kept sliding a piece of lined writing paper from one hand to the other across the table. His head bobbed, first from side to side as though he was disagreeing with me, then up and down in complete agreement.

"The bottom line, Darquel, is if this kind of thing happens again, you'll be banned from school." I tried to sound as stern as Dr. Abraham.

"And Officer O'Shay and I would really hate to see that happen."

I'm not sure what surprised me more—that the paper froze mid-shift or that O'Shay coughed out a "That's right."

Darquel was back in class the next morning, but Puma didn't come to school for a few days after. I knew that wouldn't last long. He'd be too afraid of missing something.

There weren't many places you could go to for excitement in jail. The clinic was usually pretty good. Some dude was always flipping out on the nurse about getting, or not getting, his medications. Then there was church, but all you could do there was talk in the back pews. And nothing much happened in the dayroom anymore ever since Patch beat the crap out of that snitch Alfie and broke his jaw.

School was the best. You got to see your buddies from all over the jail, talk and pass shit around even though O'Shay swore that nobody ever got anything past him. And there was always the chance some asshole would wig out in class and they'd call a code.

When Puma came back to class he firmly planted himself at the opposite end of the table away from Darquel, and waited.

But nothing happened.

Even though I was pretty sure Puma hadn't told anybody about the note (it was too much of a threat to his or anybody else's masculinity) the class was eerily quiet for the rest of the week.

Everybody moved around the classroom more deliberately.

Folders were neat; paper, pencils, and erasers were politely and promptly passed around. Everybody, including O'Shay, was careful about what they said, or said nothing at all.

Suddenly, in a place where everybody knew everything about everybody, or at least insisted they did, these boys acted like the strangers they really were to each other.

That stillness, that suspended sense of waiting didn't last long.

Cell blocks and jailhouse classrooms are about as elastic as lungs: you can only hold your breath so long before you have to let it out.

O'Shay was the first to explode.

"That's the last fuckin' warning I'm givin' your black Dominican ass, Midnight," he snarled.

They stood practically nose to nose. I could see their hands knotting into fists at their sides.

"I heard you out in the hallway cursing at Ms. Winters. You know we don't fuckin' talk that way around here. And if you don't fuckin' like it, find yourself another hole to shit in, 'cause you ain't doin' it here."

Everybody gave a sigh of relief, and instantly things were back to normal.

The jokes and gossip started up.

Dmitry and Garcia nodded off over their assignment, and Walter kept trying to copy work off of whoever sat next to him.

During that few days' hiatus, though, the room had somehow shifted. Now there was a permanent place for Darquel at the table, close to O'Shay, with Midnight on one side and my grade book and papers on the other.

Darquel still smiled, and every once in a while that crazy, haunted cackle cut through the room's clamor.

The difference was that nobody paid any attention to him, except that two or three of the guys might shake their heads and smile to themselves or give their own bemused chuckle.

The day Darquel fell to the floor the classroom was packed.

"Yo, man, whatta fuck's goin' on," a couple of the guys shouted and jumped up as though he'd spilled hot coffee on them.

Before any of the rest of us understood what was happening, O'Shay was at the phone and called a medical code.

Then, while he got all the other guys out of the room and into the hall, I pushed the table and chairs away from Darquel as his arms and legs, rigid then limp, kicked out in all directions.

Darquel grunted and choked, his jaw clenched tight around his strangled gags, his face swollen as though his tongue was a cork in a bottle.

"Roll him on his side," O'Shay shouted over his shoulder, getting the last inmate out. "Keep his airway clear."

O'Shay squatted next to me and nudged me out of the way. He leaned Darquel's twisting, moaning body against his thigh.

"Medical should be here any minute," he said, looking up at me.

"It's okay, buddy. Medical should be here any minute," he repeated, leaning over Darquel, his voice suddenly more brogue than Bronx.

"Where the goddamn fuck are they," he glowered up at me a minute later. "Goddamn sons of bitches."

Darquel whimpered, his hands groping, his lungs gasping for whatever air they could get.

"Everything's gonna be fuckin' okay, little buddy, try to take it fuckin' easy now," O'Shay cooed with the lilt of an Irish lullaby.

Darquel's body went limp, his face a sheen of sweat. Then suddenly his legs and arms thrashed out again, drool and spit spraying all over. It was as though the demons who haunted him were hissing out their own spell against O'Shay's charm of comfort.

"Yo, yo, kid, take it easy," O'Shay whispered as close to him as he could get without being hit.

"Goddamn these people," O'Shay sputtered. "Where the fuck—"

"There's a problem here, officer?" a voice interrupted.

A nurse, a tall white woman with her hair swept up in a bun, stood at the open door looking in.

I got up and moved to make room for her.

O'Shay glared at her, then he moved away a little but kept his hand on Darquel's shoulder propping him up, stroking his arm every once in a while.

But the nurse didn't move.

Instead she stayed in the doorway and clamped her arms across her brightly colored smock of red, blue, and green balloons. As she stared down at O'Shay, her jaw was as clenched as Daquel's had been, and as clenched as O'Shay's was now. He was working hard to behave himself.

"Dr. Hubbel will be here in a minute," the nurse announced, settling against the doorframe to wait.

She never touched Darquel.

She never moved to his side, never said a word of reassurance to him.

She never tried to ease him with a gentle, hovering hand.

That was left to O'Shay.

Gruff, tactless, crude, suck-it-up, tough-shit-kid O'Shay.

Turning away from the nurse, he eased in closer and hunched over the boy.

By then Darquel was as limp as an old, overused mophead, and he was just as smelly as one since he had lost what little control he usually had over his body.

Still, O'Shay cradled Darquel's lolling head in his lap and whispered to him while we waited.

I couldn't hear what O'Shay was murmuring to him through his black, chewed-up cigar stub. But whatever it was, Darquel's usual hallucinatory grimace disappeared, and the rictus from his seizures vanished, and suddenly his mouth curled into the kind of sweet but mischievous smile little boys give when they feel safe even though they know they've been a royal pain in the butt.

That smile was one shit-eating grin I was sure O'Shay was happy to see.

Chapter Seven
Addicted

The only thing Jason wasn't addicted to was school.

"I'm just not into it, man, never was. No sense starting now. Maybe when I'm upstate..." He'd let his sentence trail off.

It was a conversation we'd had a number of times. Every week or so when I went to Jason's block to do some tutoring with Jamal and Eric, two of my slowest readers, I'd make it a point to bug him about coming to class.

"Naw, man, I'm just not witit." He'd wave me away.

He wouldn't even bother to look up from his Monopoly game.

Then, as I walked away, as though he was afraid he had hurt my feelings, he'd swivel his polished, shaved head around and call over his bony shoulder, "Sorry, Mr. C."

He might not have been into school, but he was certainly into every drug going. At seventeen Jason smoked weed, loved chronic, snorted coke or glue or gasoline, popped E pills whether he was clubbin' or not, shot heroin, all in whatever combination came his way. He didn't care what the stuff was peppered with as long as it punched his insides out and numbed his wide-awake brain.

He'd recite that litany of drugs like the lyrics to his favorite rap song. You could hear him all over the block, up on the tier, on his bunk, echoing out from the shower or the bathroom, weed, chronic, coke...

Read his school records, the few there were (the kid was right, he'd never been "witit"), and you'd see he came by his addictions honestly.

His fifteen-year-old mama, Shalene, was a tiny-boned, light-skinned girl who didn't seem strong enough to hold herself up, let alone the extra weight of a baby. She indulged in everything— cigarettes, booze, weed, meth, crack, smack—while she carried him.

She couldn't tell you if that was to celebrate having a baby or to forget about the thing growing inside her belly, or wherever it was, what the hell did she know, or care, for that matter. It all meant the same thing to her, puking her guts up every morning and not being able to get into her jeans anymore. But at least pregnant, she had a lot more guys sniffing around her than before, and she liked that.

Celebration or denial—her son was born addicted to the world.

Jason was as addicted to the streets and everything that went with them as he was to his drugs. He got off on the trash, the boarded up storefronts, the patrol cars that slowly cruised the hood like hos at work, the hos he proudly called by name.

He was hooked on the smell of stale beer, of piss on the side of Manny's bodega and of the bums who never stop bugging him and his homies for spare change, or swigs from their bottles of Olde English, no matter how many times they beat the shit out of them.

And he needed the young shorties, the ones who strutted up and down those streets pretending they had somewhere real to go, the way he needed those forties. He didn't care what the bitches looked like, although he was pretty loud about big butts and titties.

"And they gotta have them tight jeans so you can see that crack," he'd talk like a pimp selling his wares. Even the old-timers on the block shook their heads at the kid's foolishness.

He'd get so loud about it that the other guys would shout him down, tell him to shut the fuck up, until Targus, the block CO, finally jumped in and shut the whole thing down.

"Wooder, another word outta you and I'm dragging your ass off to the lockdown unit myself," Targus shouted.

He was a new CO who, for some reason, had been thrown into the fire of the minor block fresh from his training at the academy. Usually it was a post only seasoned COs worked. It was probably his bulked-up frame, his height (he was over six feet five inches) and the obvious knife scar just below his right ear that qualified him.

I'd seen him in operation a few times before and knew that that scar was a good barometer of where you stood with the man. If it turned red and livid against his pale complexion, you knew you'd crossed the line.

Jason might not go to school, but he wasn't stupid. He could see the barometric pressure rising in the man, so he'd quiet down, if only for a while.

But like all junkies he'd start up again, going on about the babes that gave you those skull and crossbones glares that really said, "Come on, I'm open."

Or the young birdheads who'd giggle and look coy over their shoulders and hang on each other as they walked by, all nervous like him or one of his niggas was going to jump out and do them right there.

"Whatever, man. All I gotta say is pussy is pussy, and I gotta have it." He'd be back to shouting again like a man about to jump off a cliff.

But he insisted that he wasn't like the other guys he hung out with. He liked the wooing as well as the getting, although that's not what he called it. Ask him, and he'd tell you that all he was doing was using his charm to scheme on the chicks so he could get some of that.

If there were no shorties to scope out, he was into the cars, either the ones parked along the curb, or the ones him and his boys stole and hacked up like stockyard butchers, selling parts and pieces to Lenny's uncle's chop shop.

He was addicted to that knot of black guys standing on the corner, *their* corner, waiting, drinking forties, smoking weed, never turning their backs to the street, always looking out, keeping track of who's rolling by, in what, and why.

They didn't talk much, not even Jason. They just nodded their heads, bopped to some silent beat or the blare of music blasting from some car cruising by. Then one of them would start spitting out the words and phrases of some hip-hop song they'd absorbed, the same way language just seemed to seep into a baby's tongue.

Somewhere along the way Jason got hooked on the neighborhood old ladies.

"They bugged the shit outta the other guys." He'd smile sagely. "But not me. Them old ladies were pretty harmless. They got nothing better to do, 'cept hang out."

Like Mrs. Token who sat at her window all day because she was so fat she couldn't leave her apartment. And there was Miss Lydia, his man Walter's older sister, the one who was old enough to be his mother—and maybe was, Walter confessed to him one night when they were both totally wasted on some lightning-fast crack—who spent her days walking back and forth to the store pushing an empty laundry cart.

Jason got a kick out of those old ladies shouting at him and his boys to get a job, to stop hanging out the way their worthless daddies did, daddies nobody even remembered now.

"Man, them old bags kept yellin' at us. 'Stop selling drugs!' 'All you do is shoot each other up!' 'Leave the girls alone. We don't need no more babies to take care of.' They were piss funny."

He'd laugh at them even when they started in on how him and his buddies were wrecking their neighborhood as though it really belonged to them and not to that knot of young black men, the ones who made it what it was.

He got high off those harmless hags, unless it was one of those preacher ladies, the ones who during the day scrubbed white people's toilets and did their laundry, who then at night ranted and raved about Jesus in old, dirty, abandoned storefronts.

"Places even the crackheads didn't want," he'd spit out his revenge.

If one of those real pious ones like old Sister Goodness, done up in her long white dress and white turban, started talking all that righteous shit about "how much your mamas have done for you, you bunch of ungrateful, black ingrates," looking him right in the eye, nodding in his direction as though she knew him, knew his mama, then he had no choice.

He had to feel the white-knuckled grip of a baseball bat in his hand. He had to feel the jolt up his arm just before the car windshield smashed from his direct hit.

He'd never disrespect one of those old ladies.

"But nobody, nobody talks about my mama," he'd splutter to nobody in particular.

Jason got off on the car alarm splitting the air, whooping and beeping.

That siren, though, was just one more piece of noise in the chaos of the streets that nobody paid attention to. Why should they, nothing ever happened anyways—call 911 because your Auntie Sarah all of a sudden couldn't move her arm and was talking gibberish, and you sat there waiting, holding her hand, praying she wouldn't die on you like everybody else, until you realized the cops weren't coming and you started screaming for somebody to get a cab, real quick.

So, one more whining car alarm don't mean shit.

"Nothing happened until I'd go to the back of the car and do the same thing," he said as though reciting a well-worn formula for success.

Then the street got quiet. Everybody scattered. Suddenly they had stuff to do.

Not his boys, Tomas, Mumbles, and Walter, though.

"They knew I'd got this probation thing hanging over me."

So Tomas grabbed his hoodie. But Jason shoved him off.

"I got one of 'em in the chest, I was so pissed I couldn't see which one." Jason shook his head, surprised by his own rage. Then he gave an apologetic wave across the dayroom to Tomas who happened to look up from watching some Spanish soap on TV.

But even that blind punch felt good, as though he'd been holding his breath underwater and almost didn't make it to the surface.

It didn't stop Walter from yanking his arm, begging him to get out of there.

"You shoulda heard him, man." He stared around at his audience, kids younger than he was, just boys really, the ones who hadn't heard his stories before, his voice low, confiding, a natural storyteller.

Even though most of those guys were younger, they should've known enough not to believe anything he said. After all he was a fiender, a crackhead, and everybody knew crackheads never told the truth. They shouldn't have believed his bullshit. But they did. Every word of it.

"Com'on, man, com'on, J, the pigs'll be here any minute. If they get you this time, you're fucked," Walter kept shouting.

But his homies knew that's what he wanted. They'd seen that look before, Jason waiting for the cops, ready to goad them on, invite them to the chase.

He was addicted to the adrenaline rush.

Sometimes he outran them, his heart hammering, his blood hot in his ears and behind his eyes. His mouth would be dry, gulping down air like dope, not because he couldn't breathe but because he was laughing so hard, he was having such a good time, kicking over garbage cans, running down the aisle of the Indian market, out the back door.

"You shoulda seen those towel heads jabbering all crazy at me."

Until he'd finally crawl under some car like a mangy stray cat, until the cops gave up, grumbling to each other, "Whatta hell do we care; they fuckin' got insurance, for chrissake," and took off in the squad car.

But it didn't always work out that way.

Like this last time.

Now Jason was back at the county pen, hanging all day in the dayroom, refusing to go to school ("No offense, Mr. C"), talking his war stories to anybody who'd listen, waiting for the bus to take him up for a long stretch of state time.

That was okay with Jason because he was addicted to jail.

The COs who knew him—and they all knew him since he was in and out of lockup so much—said he was addicted to "three hots and a cot."

But he'd tell you otherwise.

The noise, the dirt, the endless games of cards and Monopoly played for the high stakes of cookies and black market cigarettes, the hours of boring TV, the shakedowns with the po-lice all decked out in their riot gear tearing the block up, screaming at them, pissed because they never found the stash they'd been tipped off about, it was all a part of his habit, along with the fights, the guaranteed violence, the hunt and strike.

But Jason didn't go for the weakest link, the baby-faced white boys on the block who never once in their lives had to fight to keep what was theirs or to scrap just to walk down the street.

"Why waste your time on some pussy you know you can beat down," he'd say, looking into the eyes of those very white boys he was talking about. But no matter what he said about them, they were still his biggest fans. They knew where their safety was.

"I like taking on the tough guys who'd been upstate big time."

He'd fight the ones who were dumb as dirt but as dirty as a state bid made you, with blood on their hands they hadn't even bothered to wash off or cover up.

He baited them the way he'd seen these guys do with bears in old movies. He liked getting to those beefed-up dudes, the ones who did two hundred push-ups in one clip, their muscles strapped to them like bombs ready to detonate. He enjoyed getting close enough to light their fuse, to crack the code, without those stupid fuckers even knowing they'd been set up.

He thrived on the plotting, the planning, the careful choreography that went into a fight. He'd get his buddies to distract Targus, which wasn't easy to do since, even though he was new, he was smart and didn't take shit.

But with the CO out of the way the two of them could spit out the ritual jailhouse challenge: "Take it to the bathroom."

He wasn't ashamed to admit that he needed the fight but not necessarily the victory.

As much as anything else, he craved the taste of blood from a busted lip, or his knuckles bruised purple from badgering his opponent's bulk and brawn.

Once the bear was trapped in a narrow shower stall, Jason got a kick out of watching him finally figure out that he'd been made the fool.

"He'd look at me, the guy's eyes getting all wide and shit, that's when he'd finally realize he'd been had," he'd snort.

That was when, with nobody around to see him do it, since all the other kids were raising hell on the upper tier keeping Targus out of their way, he kicked Jason in the balls until he threw up.

And Jason was addicted to the sour smell of his own puke, the puke searing through his nostrils like pure coke.

Then before he'd even got done wiping the puke off his face, he'd already be itching for the next fight, the next hit of power juice.

But he wasn't just hooked on the fights and brutality.

"After all I'm only a kid," he'd protest when he was finally caught pulling off some prank and the sergeant handed him a disciplinary report and thirty days lockdown.

He'd get just as zooted on plain old mischief, the kind of little boy stuff that him and his friends used to do before they discovered weed and pussy.

"We did all kinds of crazy shit like dropping pumpkins off the overpasses on the highway or filling people's mailboxes up with shaving cream."

Jail could be that kind of fun. Where else could you get forty young brothers together in one place, all pissed off, hungry for booty, bored, coming off of one drug or another. Brothers swearing that this time the judge was going to nail them good, lock them up forever, or, if they were new in the system, sure their mama or their man would bail them out any minute now, because they had mad cash. Forty young boys all wild from smuggled in weed and jailhouse hooch. It couldn't get any better than that.

Jason was addicted to the toilets stuffed up and overflowing so that Targus had to let them into the dayroom early while maintenance cleaned up the water and shit, because everybody knew you never flooded a toilet unless you had saved up a couple loads.

And he got buzzed from the all night screaming sessions when nobody could sleep, not even Remington, the eleven-to-seven CO who worked back-to-back shifts and counted on that shut-eye to make it through the next day.

Forty locked up, locked down, locked-away teenage boys screeched, shouted, sang, rap-slammed, howled at a moon they hadn't seen in months, if even then, since most of them probably hadn't bothered to look up at the night sky when they were out on the streets, they'd be too busy hustling and jiving and scoring.

But as much as Jason liked to play around, he wouldn't have anything to do with some of the schoolboy pranks the other guys pulled off.

"I may be bad, but I'm not mean," he explained to me one afternoon when he decided that he might as well talk to me instead of grunting the way he usually did since I obviously wasn't going to stop bugging him with those dayroom visits.

"I don't piss in some dorky kid's iced tea bottle, or extort cookies from the littlest kids on the block. And I don't care how bad some asshole's breath smells, I ain't doing something stupid like squeezing toothpaste under his pillow."

But after a while Jason was ready for the state bus.

"All this playtime gets boring," he'd complain.

He was looking forward to state prison, "the real thing," he'd say whenever any of the younger, newer kids asked him about it.

"Yo, holmes, I been in and out of state. And I can tell you, it's a lot better than this country club. They got way better food, more rec time, stronger weed, and tougher dudes to mess with."

The way his eyes pinpointed with excitement, you knew he got high just thinking about climbing into the back of that blue minibus with its thick, wire-meshed windows, cracked vinyl seats, and the smell of fear and rage and despair from all the men who'd made the same trek over the years.

He looked forward to the two cops hustling him and the other upstate inmates into the back of the bus. They'd all be loaded down—the COs in their bulletproof vests with at least one piece each strapped to their belts; Jason and the other guys in their ankle and wrist shackles.

"If my brain wasn't so fried I'd probably recognize those cops from my other trips upstate." He shook his head, sounding like the disapproving parent he never had.

He knew the routine. Just as the van pulled out from the county lockup heading toward the highway, the CO who rode shotgun would flip on the intercom and ask the guys in the back what kind of music they wanted to hear on the radio.

"There were always a couple of new jacks who hadn't been around. They didn't know the game. They'd throw out a favorite hip-hop station, all smiles, thinking they were gonna at least get to hear to some tunes on the way up."

Not Jason. He'd just sit back and watch it happen, because he knew that as soon as they hit the road the two pigs up front would blast old '60s and '70s crap, or if they were pissed off because some dude had busted their balls getting into the van, they'd play that classical shit.

"You should see it, right, Tomas," he'd yell over to his man who never seemed to leave the TV set his whole bid. "Those guys would go nuts, cursing, pounding on the sides of the van acting like them COs was dumping hot oil in their ears."

Not him. He knew the deal. He didn't waste his breath.

Since you never knew when the bus would come, Jason waited, and waited.

Then one day when I went to the block to tutor Jamal and Eric, Jason wasn't there.

When I asked them where he was (I figured he got himself on lockdown) Eric shook his head.

"Nope, bus came this morning. You woudn'a believed that dumb ass, Mr. C, jumping around like they was taking him to the circus or something"—and this from one of my slowest learners.

But I wasn't as incredulous as Jamal and Eric.

I could easily imagine Jason running to that van, hopping in back, spreading out on the seat, happy as a kid going on a field trip.

After all, the boy was addicted to the whole damn crazy thing.

Chapter Eight

Mirror, Mirror

Kahlil, my man, you *have* to stay in your seat and stop following me around," I said with more exasperation than I wanted to show.

Although Kahlil was a small young man—at eighteen he was no more than five-feet tall—he was muscled and compact; so more than once that morning I almost fell over him as he dogged my steps around the room.

"But, Teach, I just want to show you something," he whined too close to my ear.

"C'mon, Teach, please."

Truth was, I was ready to smack him the way an irritated parent might want to hit a demanding "I want candy" kid in the grocery checkout lane.

But Kahlil didn't want candy.

He wanted my attention.

"Just take a look at what I wrote," he persisted, waving his notebook in front of me.

"Kahlil, the teacher told you to sit down," Ramos, the CO in charge of the classroom, jumped in. It was about the tenth time that day he saved me from exploding. "Now come on, papi, have a seat."

That's the way Kahlil had been ever since he started coming to school: insistent, needy, and pesky.

When he first got arrested, he was put on the psych block where he was well-known. Ramos did overtime on G block and told me Kahlil knew all the staff by name, calling the attending psychiatrist, Dr. Abraham, "My man, Abe," as though they came from the same hood. He had a medical chart as long as some inmates' rap sheets.

He didn't seem to mind spending his days dressed in a stiff, paper, hospital gown that jail-wide was known as a "Gucci gown," watching Jerry Springer until they got his meds adjusted, pulling him up from the sump of depression, or bringing him down from the crest of euphoria.

Kahlil was known there, the way he was known by most of DOC. He'd been in and out of foster care, group homes, juvenile detention, and mental hospitals for most of his early years, and, since the age of fifteen, he'd been in and out of county corrections.

"Mr. C, have you heard of this guy?" he asked me the first day he was allowed to come to school, his mind and body in precarious balance.

He held out a copy of *The Prophet*, its cover torn off since hard-cover books were considered potential weapons.

I smiled.

Like a lot of my generation I'd carried that book around like scripture during the '60s, and since then I'd heard its more sentimental, sententious passages read at my friends' children's weddings.

"I was named after this guy," Kahlil went on, not waiting for my answer—a habit, I soon learned, I'd have to get used to.

Since Kahlil had the swarthy complexion and jet-black hair of this Middle Eastern poet, I thought maybe he was right. But I knew better than to ask him what nationality he was. Whenever I'd ask a student about his ethnic background he'd gape at me like I'd given him a strand of DNA and said, "Here, read this."

Or maybe Kahlil wasn't Middle Eastern at all. Instead, maybe he had a romantic dreamer in his background who remembered all those lines about love and named this baby boy after that hopeful philosopher.

"He's got no family," Ramos said when I asked him.

He shook his head in sad disbelief.

Ramos was a Puerto Rican who seemed blood-tied to half the Bronx.

It was true. Kahlil never talked about a mother or father, or any family, for that matter. There was no rescuing grandmother, no doting older sister, not even a swindling auntie like Crazy Ray's. There was only an uncle buried alive in some state prison for more decades than Kahlil had fingers.

On the rare occasions when Kahlil did talk about his growing up, he didn't show any of the usual bitterness about being abandoned, the way the other guys did whenever family came up.

If he mentioned people who'd been important to him, he'd talk about how a particular counselor at a group home, or a nurse at the county psych hospital had helped him out when he was having a hard time. He'd say counselor or nurse the way some people said mom or pop or grandma.

"He was a poet. Like me," he said proudly.

Kahlil was indeed an artist and a writer who took his vocation as seriously as his namesake.

Ever since I had given him one of those black-and-white marbled notebooks with the stitched-in paper, he pored over it by the hour. He crammed it full with penciled poems, unpunctuated blocks of prose, small intricate drawings, elaborate borders populated by strange creatures, and cryptic calligraphy until the pages were smeared gray from erasures and the rub of his hand.

He worked over those pages the way some other young men in jail parsed their rap lyrics with heads bobbing, cheeks and lips popping out a beat.

But for Kahlil it wasn't the promise of instant success in the music business that inspired him. Rather it was the silent pull of some mysterious, haunting vision. With his nose close to the page like some Talmudic scholar, he labored to decipher the works of God and his devils.

And there were a lot of both in those pages.

To show me how much he appreciated the notebook (I had to get special permission from the warden to give it to him since it had a cardboard cover) Kahlil insisted I read several poems.

I've read my share of adolescent poetry over the years of my teaching. Puberty seems to put a pen in every teenager's hand, one of those old-fashioned, leaky fountain pens that splotched ink all over the place, except in the case of the teenaged poetaster it was love—found, lost, lamented—that made a mess all over the page.

Kahlil's verse, however, was steeped in dark, brooding, and menacing emotions and images that most kids couldn't approach, even if they had access to them.

I was happy they didn't.

He filled page after page with a rant of paranoia and pain, visions and nightmares untouched and unhampered by medication or reality.

God and a cabal of demons played a big part in his works and world, a God who hunted and punished. Sometimes his victims were whoever Kahlil told him to prey on—the old guy who didn't have any teeth and kept stealing his breakfast banana from his tray, or the commissary lady who finally turned him in for stealing honey buns off the commissary truck, or CO Esposito who wouldn't let him take a shower after lights out like the other COs because he didn't like being in there when somebody else might walk in.

More times than not, though, the victim was himself.

And he spied devils everywhere—in the White House, the state of Israel, the courts, TV news. Like a well-trained naturalist, he scrupulously wrote and drew careful descriptions of what he saw—hooves and tails and scaly skin—which he maintained anybody could see if they got at just the right angle.

"Mr. C," he said, sidling up to me about a month after I had given him the notebook. He stood close in front of me and leaned in. He hunched his shoulders in that familiar stance of the suspicious.

"Did you ever notice that God spelled backward is..."

He stopped and looked over his shoulder around the room. "Dog?"

His eyes, brown as the cedars of Lebanon, wide with anticipation, looked up at me, waiting for my gaze to match his in astonishment at his discovery.

He wasn't the first adolescent boy to make this cryptological breakthrough. But most kids his age just thought that letter reversal was bugged, and didn't see any significance in it. There were some, though, who put a more sinister spin on that letter combination.

Brady was a pale-skinned, Irish kid, a techno-punk-grunge-heavy metal rock musician and rapper who loved offending as many people as he could. He had to work hard at it, though, since in reality he was a bright, well-mannered young man with a warm heart who was just barely able to shake off from his combat boots the dust of his middle-class family of a high school principal father and a social worker mother.

He'd shaved his head, and his arms and legs were covered with a tapestry of malevolent tattoos.

His ears, eyebrows, nose, and tongue were pierced multiple times. Since inmates weren't allowed to wear any jewelry, he kept the holes open using the broken off teeth of a comb.

"Doesn't surprise me that God spelled backward is dog," Brady would preach with the fervor of Jonathan Edwards to anybody who would listen, which usually guaranteed him a pretty good congregation since there wasn't much to do in jail, and the other guys were always willing to talk bullshit or listen to it.

"I mean, look at it, man, all that crap—God, church, religion, the cops, the whole friggin' jail—all run by dogs, chasing people down like dogs, tearing us apart like dogs."

He'd rant like some avatar of blasphemy, spit flying from his mouth the way I imagined him on some stage spewing out his musical tirades.

"So, of course, God would be the biggest dog of 'em all."

I was never sure if Brady believed what he said.

I was certain, though, that Kahlil did.

When he talked about God as dog you could hear the capital *D* in his voice and imagine the fine tracery illuminating the letter in his notebook.

The same notebook he had spent the morning waving in my face, following me around, tripping me up in his frantic attempt to get my attention, mewling like a petulant kid, "But, Teeeach, I just want to show you something."

That day after class Ramos sat me down.

"You know what Kahlil's doin', dontcha?"

"Doing?"

"Yeah. Him all over the place? Trying to get in your face?"

He was enjoying my blank, confused stare.

"He's tryin' to see himself in your glasses!" Ramos explained.

"'Cause he's always got-ta see himself or he goes nuts. Didntcha ever notice?"

He smirked and tipped his hands up with the obviousness of his insight.

I certainly had noticed that Kahlil didn't seem to have a center of gravity. He rarely sat down, and at times I wasn't sure his feet were even on the floor.

But now that Ramos mentioned it, Kahlil did seem to be constantly trying to look at his image wherever he could find a shiny surface. It wasn't an easy search since jails had very few mirrors or windows.

Most windows were too high along the top of the cement walls to see out of. If there was a window at ground level, it usually looked out at a one more cement wall or a section of the razor-wire crowned fence that ringed the county lockup.

It didn't really matter. Nobody stood and looked out of those windows. Inmates were hustled along the halls. If someone did stop to assure himself that there really was a world beyond, maybe trying to remember the feel of sunlight, or the prickly power of a driving rain, he was told to move it along by the hallway officers; and even those COs stood with their backs to the windows according to DOC regulations for that post.

There was one place, though, that did have clear and unencumbered windows that the guys could look out of.

"You do know dontcha, they never intended for this to be a classroom or any place where inmates would be?" Officer Ramos had said, taking me over to the long bank of windows on my first day assigned to this new room.

"Nobody seems to know what they planned for this place, but one thing's for sure, not even the commissioner of corrections gets a view like this one."

The room was bright and spacious, and perched over the entrance lobby of the new jail with a wide vista of the facility campus. From that row of windows, you could see several parking lots, the academy building where all DOC training was done, and the long brick sidewalk, shaded by trees, that visitors used when they came up from the gate or left the building.

In the distance you could make out the fields that had been a part of the original 1914 penal work farm.

It was out in those fields that criminals were rehabilitated by farming the rich soil of the Hudson River Valley, growing crops to sell, and so fill the coffers of their state keepers.

At least that's how I'd had it explained to me by more than one old-timer, those sages of jail lore and history, who, for all I knew, were second or third generation inhabitants of the place.

That dark past, however, didn't take away from the beauty of the faraway meadows and hills.

But my students didn't flock to those windows for the view when they came into the classroom.

They didn't care about scenery, they never had, since for many of them brick, mortar, and steel were the building blocks of their neighborhoods.

And they weren't interested in weather either.

"Man, I hate this weather," I remember hearing Kendrill complain. He was a tall cutout of a seventeen-year-old, whose mahogany skin made his orange DOC scrubs glow like a lit pumpkin. He had the grace of an athlete and the energy of a ballplayer out on the court.

"Look at it, sun shinin', all hot and shit."

"What are you talking about, Kenny?" I asked, feeling as though I'd missed something.

"It's beautiful out. Don't you want to have outdoor rec? You can shoot some hoops."

"I'm not going out." He sighed and shook his head.

"It just reminds me what I'd be doin' if I were out there, hanging with my boys, drinking a forty, checking out the shorties in their tight cutoffs."

Shorties.

That's what pulled them over to those windows.

It didn't make a difference what girl they spied coming up that pathway. It could be the one dragging a toddler by the arm; or the girl shouting and cursing into her cell phone while she tried to light a cigarette; or the two young women walking side by side, laughing and bumping hips.

"Yo, yo, check out that fattie," Jerome would sputter. "What a butt!"

He'd pound his man Twain's arm as though that was the only way he could siphon off all his sexual energy. Who knows? If he didn't he might've propelled himself out the window and down the walk.

Then instantly they'd all be clambering over each other, shoving for a place at the windows, moaning and covering their eyes, not believing that such beauty—"Fuck man! Such booty!"—could be out there without them.

"Hey, hey, papis, get away from there," Officer Ramos would chide them halfheartedly since he knew (having been one of them himself) that young men usually do what they were going to do until whatever mischief they were involved in has run itself out.

"You're fogging up my windows, my glasses, everything, with your heavy breathing," he'd call over from his desk exaggerating his Puerto Rican accent, the one he used when he wanted to distract them from their latest tomfoolery.

"Look at youse, your tongues all hanging out."

"Yo, CO, you gotta see this one, she's real thick," Alex or Isaac or Rommel or Hector would shout over to him, barely able to pry their eyes from the view.

"Com'on, papi, you know I'm a married man." Ramos would laugh and make them laugh, too.

We'd all watched him flirting with Sergeant Higgins, the blonde who always smelled like a fresh shower no matter what time of day, when she came up to sign his census book.

Kahlil was right there with them. He jostled to get a better view, he pushed to get closer, he took his turn fogging up Ramos's windowpanes scoping out the titties on that one or the fat ass on the other.

But Kahlil wasn't only interested in the shorties.

As much as he wanted to check out the babes, he just as much wanted to check himself out. So eventually he'd give his place up and move off to a corner of the window where the building came up and the sunlight was blocked and he could get a reflection of sorts.

There in his own private corner he'd stare at his face until Ramos started yelling.

"The wardens see you hoodlums at those windows? With your hands in your pants? I'm outtafa job," Ramos complained.

Then finally losing patience he roared, "I'll write youse up, all of youse, if youse don't get away from there."

"You right, CO, you right. We don't wanna get you in no trouble." Kahlil would snap out of his trance.

"You my man, Ramos. We go way back, you and me. You look out for me."

Ramos did and always had. He'd talk to the sergeant to get Kahlil off lockdown when he'd done something stupid. He'd make sure Kahlil had clean orange scrubs or slipped him some extra state cookies because Ramos knew he had nobody to put money on his books for commissary.

Eventually they'd drag themselves away from the windows.

But not even Ramos's threats and Kahlil's loyalty to him could stop him from scouring the rest of the classroom for some other surface that would bounce his image back to him.

Everybody knew Kahlil was vain. All you had to do was track his hairstyle from day to day, from week to week to know that.

One day he'd come to school with his long, black hair in a tightly coiled braid; on another he'd divide his locks up into three ponytails that bounced like the tassels on an exotic dancer. Or he'd pull the hair back from his face with a string of yarn from an unraveled sock and let his hair fly around behind him.

The other kids didn't mock Kahlil's vanity or laugh at him or make wisecracks about his style statements the way they did with each other. They were too wary of that fierce, feral look that darted in and out and around the edges of his eyes.

And although they may have been cautious around Kahlil, they also had a certain respect and affection for him. He was cool, he wasn't pussy. All his cuts and bruises and black eyes attested to that.

They knew he was afflicted with his own demons, demons they were happy to let someone else battle. So, they listened when he'd start on one of his harangues, and they'd read the latest poem he shoved into their hands. They told him he was lookin' good, which always brought a big broken-toothed smile to his face.

But when he started on those other restless, angry prowls around the room, stalking his furtive self in a window or a computer screen, or a polished stainless steel panel on a door they knew that this wasn't just vanity.

Suddenly the other guys would get busy with schoolwork, or start talking to the guy next to them, or pull out of their pocket some letter they'd already read a hundred times.

They'd do anything to avoid catching his gaze, because they instinctively knew exactly what Ramos was talking about. They might not understand it, but they recognized that there was no Kahlil behind that gaze. He only existed out there, as an image in your eyes or in the TV screen behind your back, or, as in my case, my eyeglasses. Ramos was right. Kahlil would maneuver me around, this way or that, always trying to position me so that the light fell just right on my lenses. Or if that didn't work, he'd scheme a way to get me in front of a computer monitor. Then he'd fix his gaze over my shoulder and lock his eyes with his own mirrored likeness.

Those times, he wasn't talking to me but instead to his reflection, and I was the one who felt that I didn't exist.

When I finally tried to move away, or said that it was time for him to sit down and get some work done, I could see the panic in his eyes. It was as though I'd threatened his life.

"Com'on, Teach, I just want to tell you something," he'd beg, his blank stare locked with his counterpart over my shoulder.

Then, Kahlil would make one last desperate effort. He'd twist and squirm around me, he'd shuffle from side to side as though we were partners trapped in a macabre dance, and I could see him struggling not to grab my shoulders and hold me in place.

Eventually he'd just give up, flop down exhausted on a chair like a doll bereft of its stuffing, and put his head down on the desk, his notebook and arm a pillow, and fall into a deep sleep.

Then, the room would become quiet and still, the only sounds, the whispered sighs of pencils against paper and the rustle of Ramos's *Daily News*.

Kahlil would twitch like an animal asleep, his outstretched hand groping the empty air, searching, reaching for a pen, the magician's wand, the devil's pitchfork, or maybe even God's own hand.

Chapter Nine

Children of Disappointment

It wasn't hard to figure out what we were all in for the first day Ms. Wharton took up her new post as second floor hallway officer in the new jail where I had one of my classrooms.

"Don't you look at me that way," I could hear her growl yelp through the safety-glass window where she sat at a desk just outside my room.

"Don't stand there; move when I tell you," her voice soft and low no matter how hard she tried to pitch it.

"I wasn't talking to you, mister," she spit out. "Move your ass out of the hallway before I call security on you."

Ms. Wharton hated what she did and everybody else along with it.

She was rude to the medical staff and to me and the other teachers, and she screamed at the inmates, cutting them with a nasty wit as sharp as the creases in her blouse. She routinely denied the men's requests for the barber, the medication nurse, an extra ten minutes in the law library. She was quick to write inmates up for minor DOC infractions.

And she had her own book of rules as well. Break one of them and she skipped the paperwork and had your block officer lock you in for the day. Forget about appealing to the CO. He'd do whatever she told him to. Nobody would stand up to her mouth.

It didn't help that Ms. Wharton was a short, full-breasted, pretty young woman with smooth, toffee-colored skin and big, almost black eyes in a place with nothing but steel and stone and hundreds of men.

She looked no more than nineteen and carried herself like a rookie fresh out of the training academy. Her uniform was always neat and pressed beyond regulations, and her embroidered DOC patch looked newly stitched on her sleeve.

But as much as she hated the inmates, they loved her. They got a kick out of her spunky, sassy attitude.

"Um, um, umm, little lady's really carrying on today," I'd hear the older men, gray and stooped from too many years locked up or on the streets, chuckling, whispering to each other.

"Wipe that smirk off your face, old man," she'd snarl.

"Yes, ma'am."

"Sorry, ma'am."

The louder and more unreasonable she got, the more polite and attentive they became.

"Let me get that for you, Ms. Wharton."

"Whatever you say, ma'am. You right."

All of which made her madder.

Even the young guys I taught, who ordinarily were quick to take on the slightest challenge to their limited freedom and fragile male dignity, were able to put up with her random and arbitrary spurs. Usually.

Still there were times when their rage would be unleashed by Officer Wharton's.

"Fuckin' bitch." The classroom door would explode open. "She can fuckin' write me up. I'll fuck the bitch up."

Luckily, the other guys would help out.

They'd all been there.

"Man, you know what the bitch is like. You keep shoutin' like that and she'll call a fuckin' code and have the goon squad up here all over your ass."

Yet, as quick as it happened it was over.

One minute they'd be cursing her out, chewing over their own beefs with her, and the next minute they'd be falling out of their seats, hands deep inside the front of their pants, eyes glued to the hallway window, watching her walk down the hall.

"Man, look at that big butt."

"I'm gonna get me some of that."

"She's hot," they'd call and respond to each other across the room.

It might not have taken me long to figure out that Ms. Wharton hated what she did and everybody with it. It did take me a while, though, to realize that her indifference to me had a lot more edge to it than the usual DOC lack of cordiality.

Her first few weeks there, I'd get off the elevator every morning with my bag of books, walk down the hall past her desk, and smile.

"Morning, Officer Wharton." I'd nod, then slouch against the window to let her know I wasn't rushing her to unlock my door.

"Been a good morning so far?"

The first few times she didn't answer I figured she was preoccupied. Officer Gomez from my new jack days back when I first started to work at corrections had taught me that there was a lot of jailhouse bustle in the morning—breakfast trays, medications, getting the inmates out for county court.

I don't know how many "good morning"s were left hanging in the air like an open palm extended for a handshake before I got the point: I wasn't significant enough to be even snarled at. You have to *exist* before you can be discarded. She looked right through me—that is, when she didn't turn her back to me.

Once class started there'd be times during the day when I had to send a student back to his block for some reason, or had to check with her about some DOC procedure.

I'd stick my head out the door, the latch loudly clacking to let her know I was there, and wait.

I never interrupted what she was doing, even if it was nothing more important than filling in 14 down, "container for beer or gunpowder." I'd stand there, half in the room and half in the hallway.

"Ah, excuse me, Officer Wharton?" I'd eventually break the silence, forced to talk to her back.

"I'm sorry to bother you, but when you get a chance, Mikal

needs to go back to the block?" I'd simper like a supplicant at the altar of some fierce goddess.

Minutes would tick by with no acknowledgment that she had even heard me. Then, without turning in my direction, she'd say over her shoulder, "Send him out."

The guys were right: the woman *was* a bitch.

Obviously she didn't like me.

But I knew I couldn't let her get to me. It was the same advice I'd give to the guys in my class.

Instead, I decided to take her on. She became my mission.

After all, I was brought up a 1950s Roman Catholic and, like many of my generation, was taught by the nuns and priests to crave a challenge. At some time or other, all my friends and I wanted to be missionaries and spent a good part of our elementary school days learning about the atrocities endured by the nuns at the hands of the filthy pagans in such heathen countries as the Belgian Congo.

We loved it.

It helped that we had been raised on the lives of the martyrs. We read about them, heard about them from the pulpit, saw them on the big screen. We even discussed the worse torture to be endured. For me, it was the dentist drill. Secretly I always felt it was a safe choice since I assumed they didn't have electricity in darkest Africa, and they certainly didn't have dentist drills.

I gave myself six months. I might not be able to convert Officer Wharton to liking me by then, but at least I'd get her to look at me when I talked to her.

Besides, she was nothing compared to a whirling dentist drill going for an exposed nerve.

Well, most days she wasn't.

I didn't change my approach much at first. I didn't want to give myself away. I worried that if I ratcheted up the kindness she'd see what I was doing. Not only that, I knew how enraged she got when some of the men made an effort to be nice to her.

Instead, I just didn't give up.

I'd seen how the nurses and maintenance men dealt with her: say what you had to say, ask for as little as possible, do your job; that was the strategy.

Even her colleagues kept their distance. Officers might stop at her desk to complain about the day's duty sergeant or to look over the local paper she always brought in. Occasionally, there'd be some article that created a buzz: county taxes, a big drug bust, a CO who had been arrested for some kind of scam (something that happened all too often). But even those conversations took place mostly around her and over her.

So, I kept doing what I was doing. The smile wasn't wider, the good morning wasn't brighter, but at least it was still there.

And Officer Wharton kept doing what she was doing.

Except at first she stepped up her campaign of hostilities.

Who knows? Maybe she had her own timetable, and estimated that by now I was supposed to have rejected her like everyone else, and hadn't, so she better get serious about it.

Doors stayed locked longer.

She complained that the classroom was messy, that I wasn't following the schedule—dismissal time for lunch was 11:15 not 11:30.

And getting her attention became an endless chant of "Excuse me, Officer Wharton."

Then I made my own counterattack.

I looked for ways to meet her complaints. All schoolwork was done by 11:05 a.m. My students emptied the wastebasket and swept the floor after both sessions.

Instead of hanging out of the door to ask her something, I wrote my requests on slips of paper and put them on her desk.

"For when you have time," I'd apologize.

When that didn't work I decided to make a message box I could drop requests into. That way she didn't have to look at me. We could both continue to pretend I didn't exist.

I brought in an old Timberland shoebox and asked one of my

students, Christian, an accomplished graffiti artist who tagged old freight cars in the Bronx, to design it.

"Yo, Mr. C, are you sure you want to sacrifice a *Timberland* box?" he joked when he saw the Timberland tree, one of the icons of his generation.

"You know how Ms. Wharton is. She'll probably torch it just by looking at it."

You would think I had brought in free Timberlands for everybody the way the other guys passed that box around, nostalgic for their own boots and the feel of the streets beneath them.

They all started giving Christian suggestions.

Alex, an acne-scarred white kid, claimed that Ms. Wharton's favorite color was green.

"No really, I know," he whined over the razing he got.

"Oh yeah, lover boy," Andre, who was as black as Alex was white, jumped in. "Whatcha do, see the color of her thong when she bent over to tuck you in?"

Everybody laughed including Alex who blushed pink. For once they seemed to have Ms. Wharton where they wanted her, the brunt of their jokes but at the same time the object of their lusts.

The final product was a masterpiece.

Christian made the box look like a train car. It was done in shades of green with "Ms. W's In-Box" bold on the side. There were all manner of cats peeking around the letters because Jose knew, he just *knew* ("Don't ask me how, man," he joked using a fake *Comedy Central* Latino accent) she loved cats.

I wasn't sure how to get the in-box to her. It couldn't be a gift, and I certainly didn't want to appear to be telling her how to do her job.

In the end, Alex's innocence saved me.

"Mr. C, if you want me to, I'm going back to the block and I can drop it on Ms. Wharton's desk," Alex announced, scooping it up and heading out the door before I had a chance to say anything.

Of course nobody believed Alex when he came in after lunch

and announced that Ms. Wharton giggled when he dropped the message box on her desk.

"I swear to God, Mr. C," he insisted over the heckling of the other guys. "I sorta dropped it on her desk. I didn't say anything. She was screaming at Antonio for not having his pass, *again*, and when she turned around, it was there, and she giggled.

"I bet I saved Antonio's ass from getting written up."

"You sure she wasn't giggling at that scrawny white ass of yours hanging out of your county scrubs," Antonio jabbed back.

"No, man, she friggin' giggled," Alex snapped back, but quickly smiled because he could see it wasn't going his way.

Then, late that afternoon, I got a call from the block that Dante had an attorney visit. I hung up the phone and told him. Then I wrote out the request and moved toward the door.

This was it, the first request for the new in-box, and everybody knew it.

As I pulled open the door, the guys held their breath like the Greeks in their wooden horse.

Giggle or no giggle, I was relieved to see that the box was still there, precisely placed on the outer edge of her desk.

She was "busy" reading the newspaper, so I dropped my request into the box.

She didn't look up.

She turned the page.

The door closed.

I don't know how many minutes passed but enough to make us all feel the message box was a failure.

Through the hallway window, we could see her rustling the newspaper.

Then the room erupted.

"That bitch is cutting into my legal time," Dante paced. "It's not right; she's doin' her usual shit."

Antonio started in on Alex all over again. This time Alex knew he had to match his threats.

"Fuck you, fat boy," Alex spit out.

"Shit, white boy, you can't do shit to me." Antonio glared at Alex across the desk.

All of a sudden, Ahmed and Barak, two Five Percenters who usually only talked to other gang members, and certainly not to the "white devil," stepped over to Alex's table.

"Yo, bro, excuse us"—Ahmed met Antonio's stare—"but the young brother is only telling the truth about you and your pass."

Derek, who came from the same hood as Antonio, stood up, all six feet three inches of him, and faced them.

I often spent part of my day building firewalls, but today's threat seemed ready to jump the trenches.

I knew what was operating here.

These young guys were raised on disappointment: nobody ever did what they were supposed to do, nobody ever did what they promised they'd do. At one time or another they'd all been that little boy waiting at the window for Daddy, who swore he'd be there this weekend; or the little kid who wouldn't take off the sneakers the group home got him because Mommy promised she'd come and see his new Jordans.

They'd bought into what they believed was my promise—that this personalized in-box would win Ms. Wharton over, that she'd finally be nice and see them for the little kids they really were, hurt and bitter from waiting, from wanting to be loved.

"So much for your bullshit kindness," their bluster and threats shouted out at me. "We coulda told you nothing ever changes."

There was going to be a riot in my room any minute now, and she was going to let it happen.

Then she'd call a code and the emergency response team would arrive.

Kids would be kicked and punched and thrown into disciplinary lockup; all so she came out the winner.

The woman was a real nasty bitch.

"Excuse me, Mr. C, Dante has an attorney visit?" Officer

Wharton called through the opened door. "I would've called him sooner but the sergeant had me on the phone."

Nobody moved, not even Dante.

We stared at her back as she softly closed the door.

Dante broke the spell.

"Sorry, Mr. C, I didn't mean to start nothing. I'm real stressed about court tomorrow."

Then Alex told Antonio to forget it and gave Ahmed and Barak a weak gapped-tooth smile.

Antonio nodded at Derek and turned back to the computer.

I tried not to smile triumphantly.

Officer Wharton had never called me Mr. C. (She'd never called me anything.)

And she never apologized.

After Dante left I filled the room's awkward silence up with last minute instructions about the homework assignments, then dismissed the class.

As they were leaving, Ahmed and Barak replaced their usual sullen nod with a "Night, Teach." And Derek smiled and gave me a thumbs-up. "Good job, Mr. C."

I'd like to say that things kept getting better after that with Officer Wharton. But it was more like teaching run-on sentences to Alex. After an arduous lesson with example after example, he'd leave beaming with success until the next day when he'd come back to class barely able to remember what we talked about. Things didn't always stick.

It wasn't quite that bad with Officer Wharton.

She'd still glower, scream, and complain.

Some days I'd be transparent, nameless, a nuisance.

But other days I'd be Mr. C, and my students were quickly shepherded to visits and clinics.

But no matter what dip we were in on the road, that message box stayed on her desk.

I don't remember when exactly it happened, but after a while

Ms. Wharton started lingering in the doorway after unlocking my room in the morning. She might ask if I needed anything or might question me about a student or some school procedure; and she always told me what happened on the blocks the night before.

"They said at briefing this morning that Antonio had a fight and got his lip split open; so, *he'll* be nastier than usual," she'd report with an exasperated smile.

Eventually, she started coming into the room while I set up for the day. She'd lean against the filing cabinet and chat—there was no other word for it, her voice, light and birdlike.

"I've been working here ten years, and I've hated every minute of it," she announced one morning, then paused as though she expected me to be surprised at her unhappiness.

"I was twenty-one and was gonna go to nursing school, but then my mother got sick, lupus, so I had to work to help out with the other kids since the old man wasn't around," she'd ramble, sometimes talking to my back as I wrote on the board or got textbooks from the closet.

She expected very little from me—a nod, a smile, a question just to let her know I had a firm grip on the threads of her life story.

Because it was always her life story.

It might be something tragic, like the car crash that killed her youngest sister five years ago. ("And the guy that was driving? Walked away.")

Most times, though, it was the simple, ordinary fabric of life, like the tuna pizza she had ("Everybody says it's good, but I told them it sounded weird.") or the latest episode of some TV reality show.

That's when I learned that, indeed, Alex was right: green was her favorite color and was the color of her new Honda CRV, and the new drapes in her living room.

"Everybody says I'm crazy, but I'm gonna paint my bathroom myself," she declared one day, "and it's gonna be green, of course."

After a while I began to wonder who the "everybody" was she talked about. Despite her new comfort with me, she still cut people short and people avoided her.

So, whoever these "everybody"'s were, they were nameless.

The only names she dropped were those of the stray animals she took care of at the local animal shelter where she volunteered every day after work.

"That's why I won't work overtime. They get enough blood outta me here," she countered, as though I were a sergeant waving a time sheet in her face.

She told me about the litter of tabby kittens, hours old, thrown into a trash barrel. Or the golden retriever blinded by kids throwing rocks.

"*Those* are the people who should get the electric chair," she fumed, ready to throw the switch herself.

"I don't understand how people can be so cruel," was her daily refrain. "What do they get out of it?"

Then one morning Ms. Wharton was late for work.

Officer Parsons, a sour man who was always praising the Lord while brewing hellfire for nonbelievers, was pulled off the elevator to work the hallway.

"She's always crabbing about me to the sergeant, but look at her, where's her? Eh?" I knew better than to break the civilian code of silence. "Didn't even bother to tell nobody she'd be late."

I wasn't there when Officer Wharton eventually came in. But I could feel her icy presence as the hallway's easy-going morning buzz stopped suddenly.

"I don't care how many complaints headquarters writes against me." She charged into my room at lunchtime. "I'm not driving by there again. I don't care if it does make me late.

"Last night when I was coming home from the shelter," she went on to explain, "this asshole in front of me runs over a baby rabbit, and never stops."

She shuddered.

"I almost threw up. I didn't want to stop, but I made myself. I mean, what if it was still alive?"

She had been late that morning because she had to drive a longer way to work so she wouldn't see that dead rabbit on the side of the road.

For the rest of the afternoon she was vicious.

Alex never made it back from the bathroom. She had him locked down because he shouted hello down the hall to his social worker.

"That's it," she screamed into my room after that. "Nobody goes to the bathroom. Shit in your pants for all I care."

Then Wilfredo got pulled out of class for a full body search. Ms. Wharton insisted that he slipped "something" into his pants.

I got my share of reprimands: too noisy, too many students roaming the room.

At the end of the day, before she left, she stood in my door.

"I couldn't get that poor rabbit out of my mind all day long. I just couldn't."

I wasn't sure if this was an apology, but I decided to take it that way.

"I hope everything goes all right," I said, knowing it made no sense to wish her a good evening.

Driving home, I couldn't get out of my mind the picture of Ms. Wharton standing on the roadside in her crisp uniform staring down at the dead rabbit, crying.

And there was another picture that wouldn't leave me. Ms. Wharton screaming into my room, "Shit in your pants for all I care."

She was on time the next morning.

She didn't say anything about the rabbit except that Sergeant Portal, a compact, muscular, no-frills woman whom everyone liked, inmates and staff alike, because she was fair, had called a friend in public works who had promised to have the carcass removed.

Officer Wharton didn't yell that day or for several weeks after. She still did her job, but she wasn't as fiercely deliberate about it as she usually was. What casualties there were—lockdowns, searches, disciplinary write-ups—were more like inevitable forces of nature—the blown down tree or the flooded stream—than acts of will.

Because she seemed to have very little will during those weeks. She moved through her day as though she was still on that roadside, stunned and wondering who could have so cavalierly wounded such a helpless creature.

Then one afternoon, before I locked up for the day, she came in and thanked me for my concern.

"You know? When the rabbit got killed," she said.

Eventually she seemed less haunted. The truce of grief was over. Battle lines were firmly drawn, and Officer Wharton was back in action.

"That Ms. Wharton, she be herself again," Saul, the barber, said to me one day. He was an old-timer who claimed the only reason po-lice kept locking him up was because he was the best barber they'd ever had.

"She be tearin' those young bucks of yours up, right and left."

This time she dug deeper into the archives of forgotten rules and got the inmates on all kinds of technicalities.

"White boxers only."

"I told you, no slippers outside the block."

"In my hallway it's full body pat down going in *and* out of all areas at *all* times. Yes, Mr. Wise Ass, including the classroom."

She still took time out from the frontline to report to me about her life.

There was the cockatoo at the shelter who had lost most of its feathers from malnutrition; the new bathroom vanity that wouldn't fit; the neighbor she reported to the police for making too much noise.

Then, a little after Thanksgiving ("The cats at the shelter loved the turkey I cooked for them," she boasted), two startling pieces of news: Ms. Wharton was going back to school part-time to become a veterinary assistant, and she was going to the Bahamas over Christmas.

"Delores? At the shelter? She got a great package for her and her friend, Mindy, for the Paradise Island Resort," she told me, her eyes already sparkling with sun and sand. "Then this Mindy canceled, and Dolores was like, looking for somebody to take the ticket, so I told her count me in.

"I figured what the hell, especially with school starting in January."

The weeks before her trip were a pendulum of pleasure and pain, a mad swing between what she would pack and the boxer puppies that had been brutalized; what she would wear and the ferret whose leg had been chewed off by a pit bull; how much she would gamble at the casinos and the twin rabbits left on the shelter doorsteps.

It turned out that Ms. Wharton hadn't traveled much. What little she did was to her mother's relatives in Mississippi.

"I hated it," she told me, barely able to wait until the guys were out of the classroom to start talking about her trip again.

"Down South? You've never seen such dirty people. Not that they could help it. But a pit for a toilet? And mama tryin' to get me pickin' beans on one of them farms for pennies? No, thank you," a little bit of the delta silting into her voice.

Her final day before the trip, Ms. Wharton studied the resort's brochures, hardly moving from her desk except to ask me every hour to check the weather on the internet.

At the end of the day as I was getting ready to leave, I saw her wipe down her desk. Then she carefully locked her message box up in the bottom drawer with a key she had on her personal key ring.

"Now don't get jealous when you get my postcard," she shouted to me as I got into the elevator. "There I'll be, on the beach, while you're slaving away in this dump."

Officer Wharton had been gone five days when Sergeant Portal greeted me first thing in the morning.

"Mr. C, something came for you in the mail." She grinned. "It's a postcard from Judy."

"Judy?"

"Officer Wharton?" She impatiently answered my quizzical look. "In the Bahamas?"

The postcard was the kind you got free in your room. It showed a ten-story white stone hotel in dazzling sunlight, with a dazzling blue sky, and a dazzling white sandy beach.

Across the back Ms. Wharton had scrawled a message.

Can't stop to talk, gotta go!

Place OK, except Dolores snores and it's rained three days and the prices are too high and the foods terrible. See you soon.

Ha-ha! Judy

I was surprised that she sent me a postcard. I hadn't expected it. After all, who was I? Just some guy she worked with, some guy she talked to a few minutes a day.

Then again, I wondered, was there really anybody else for her to send postcards to? Sergeant Portal, maybe. The strays at the shelter?

Before I put the card in my backpack to get ready for my morning class, I turned the card over and reread her message with its breathlessness, its forced joviality, its list of complaints—and that taunt, *Ha-ha!*

I wasn't sure who the joke was on. Me? My lonely locked-up boys? All the other COs yoked to their posts, counting the hours until their next day off, their next vacation, their next life?

If I had shown it to the guys in my class they would've gotten it right away because they knew that Ms. Wharton was just another child of disappointment like them, and like them, nothing ever worked out in life. Her mother got sick. Her father dumped them. She had to drop out of college and become a stupid CO. Her sister was killed. People brutalized helpless animals.

Of course Dolores ended up snoring, they would've said, and prices were too high and the weather was lousy and the food was awful. What did you expect? That's the way it had to be, because that's the way it's always been.

And that closing *Ha-ha!?*

She was letting me know that she had figured it out—that like all children of disappointment, she'd once again been had, she'd once again fallen into that impossible dream of happiness, this time in the Bahamas. That *Ha-ha!* was her way of telling me not to worry. It wasn't going to happen again. And when she got home, I could damn well be sure she'd be back on top of her game.

Chapter Ten

The Things They Carried

They didn't leave you with much when you got locked up at the county penitentiary. By the time you got to booking, you'd long lost whatever dignity you carried in with you from the streets. All you had left was your height, weight, hair, and name, and not always that.

More than once I'd had a kid explain to me as I was filling out his papers for school that his name wasn't really Abel Howard, say, the way it was listed on the daily prison census. Rather it was Howard Abel. The people in booking were usually too tired from working a double shift to get it right, or to care.

Or maybe it was an alias, thought up at the last minute.

With your hands cuffed behind your back and your face slammed against the hot hood of the cop car (the guys said this is called "resisting arrest"), the name of that scrawny cousin down in Louisiana—the one who ripped you off for some weed that summer when your mama sent you there to stay out of trouble—came to you, and you ended up serving your bid trying to remember that you were Sam Marquise and not Lloyd Palmer.

The things you carried in with you were taken away.

Clothes, sneakers, earrings, even eyeglasses, which supposedly you'd get back once you were assigned a housing block but most times didn't, because they usually got mangled somewhere between the precinct and the jail.

They took it all and locked it up as your "property."

You were allowed to carry only what they issued you: one orange uniform, one pair of slip-on blue canvas sneakers, and an ID.

Those IDs were considered more insult than possession, though. They documented one of the worst times in your life, your identity and misery laminated in plastic and stored in countless data banks across the country.

Occasionally one of the guys would laugh about his ID picture, the way some people will joke ruefully about their driver's license photo.

"I look like the village idiot," Paul quipped one day, coming up to my desk to pick up his ID before heading back to his block.

"You got that right." Antonio laughed, looking over Paul's shoulder. But Antonio quickly pocketed his own card, not wanting anybody to see the hollow-eyed boy arrested fresh from a crack house.

"Ah, the beauty of drugs," Paul skewered himself, staring down at his picture.

That wasn't the usual reaction.

Most guys guarded their IDs as though they were maps to a hidden drug stash.

But they weren't protecting any riches. They were hiding their utter poverty, ruthlessly captured at that moment, all looking tired and worn out, shocked and bewildered, some barely holding back tears of sadness or rage.

If you lost that ID, that bell of the leper, that scarlet letter, you faced a twenty-five dollar fine and thirty days lockdown, thirty days of twenty-three-hour isolation: you, your bunk, your cell door with a six-inch window, and your new ID—with, of course, the same pitiful picture.

There was one thing, though, that DOC could never take away from an inmate—a tattoo. Whether he came in with it or got it inside, he carried it with him throughout his bid.

And although corrections imposed serious penalties on the guys that got tattoos in jail and on the artists that did them ("Shit, man," I heard one of those jailhouse tattoo artists say, "the way police see it, when we do our shit, we're defacing county property"), they couldn't do anything to stop it.

I had no argument with the DOC's ban on tattoos. But I did disagree with their reasoning.

To corrections, all tattoos were, in some way or other, gang-related. As far as they were concerned, a tattoo either said to another inmate, "I'm one of you" or, more dangerously, "I'm not." Or they saw them as a silent but powerful way of telling society to "go fuck yourself."

So, one of the first things that happened in booking when a man was brought into jail was that he was told to strip down and was checked over for tattoos. Under a new gang unit sergeant, if he had any, each one was photographed, cataloged, and filed away.

I experienced those files firsthand.

Since the department automatically considered us civilians inadvertent accomplices to gang-related behavior—as far as they were concerned we were always doing stupid things—we were required to attend periodic workshops on gang behavior even though we never heard anything new. By the time I met Eddyberto I'd already been through the training a ton of times.

Sergeant Vallain had just started that year as the head of the gang unit and ran all the classes. He was a short, doughy-faced man in his thirties with wire-framed glasses who approached his work with the fervor of a tent revivalist. He lectured us on the history of gangs, the dress and gestures of gangs, and showed slides of gang graffiti.

We were warned about the dangers of giving out red pencils (Bloods) and urged to report any inmate that drew crowns over his name (Latin Kings) or capitalized all the Cs in his writing (Crips). The sergeant even went so far as to insist we report any inmate who showed an interest in Malcolm X.

"Not many of you may know this, but Malcolm X gave rise to the infamous radical Islamic gang, the Five Percenters," Sergeant Vallain informed us.

Then we were shown notebooks that Sergeant Vallain and his men had assembled of photographs of all the tattoos inmates came in with. Some of them were clearly related to gangs: the teardrop, or drops (depending on how many murders, or "bodies" the inmate laid claim to) under the eye; the skull and crossbones; the name of some neighborhood posse.

But even if a tattoo wasn't obviously gang-related, we were told it *was* nonetheless. It was just a matter of time before the gang unit figured out how.

I was disturbed flipping through those carefully assembled albums, looking at page after page of naked flesh. Shoulders, backs, necks, thighs, calves, ankles, fingers etched with intricate designs, names, and symbols, all exposed to the lens, and us. In many of the shots you could just make out a face in profile, a chin, a mouth, an ear, a hank of hair.

I felt sordid, as though I was betraying a basic human code, especially since I recognized some of those tattoos—and body parts—as belonging to guys I taught.

But I had to admit that maybe it was only *my* code that had been violated. Every once in a while, looking at those photos, I'd see a satisfied smirk on one of the faces. I suspected that some of the men were just as proud of their tattoos and their defiance of the gov'ment, as the COs were of their accomplishments in documenting all those gang emblems.

Whether I agreed or not with DOC, I still flinched whenever a student came into class with his upper arm, the back of his hand shiny with Vaseline, a sure sign that a tattoo was freshly done.

I wasn't so much concerned with his affiliations, although I knew they certainly had an impact on his life in and out of prison. I worried more about the insanity of getting tattooed in the filthy jail environment.

These guys certainly knew about HIV. Too many of them had lost family members to AIDS. And they all knew about blood and body fluids, and certainly about sharing dirty needles. But like all young people, in and out of the system, they were damn sure that death wouldn't dare stop the joyride they were on.

So, I wasn't surprised one day when Edgar came into class with the inside of his forearm shiny and sore-looking with one of the more elaborate skin designs I'd seen done in the place.

Most times, Edgar never said a word in class. He'd recently come from Mexico and was ashamed of his English and the slight speech impediment that made him swallow his words. He never called attention to himself. I suspect it was a skill he developed on the streets running a successful chop shop. Usually he was content to sit in class, do his work, and laugh at everybody else's antics.

But that day he didn't need any English. He strutted around my room with his arm on display, his swagger saying it all. "Yo! Look at me."

"Edgar, are you stupid?"

Usually, I'd never think of using a word like that around someone like Edgar, but I was mad about all the dangers he'd put himself in.

"You know you can get an infection or even HIV from doing that stuff in here," I snapped. "And besides, if you'd been caught? You could've gotten more jail time. You were damn lucky the judge gave you only eighteen months in the county pen instead of the five years state time the DA was pushing for. All that for a stupid tattoo."

It didn't matter. He still insisted on showing me his arm.

It was an etching of a heart pierced by a sword-like cross entwined with chains. One of the chain's links was shattered by a series of red drops coming from a wound in the heart. The workmanship was so fine, I couldn't help asking him how exactly it was done.

"Don't know." He smiled, rotating his arm like a pig on a spit.

"You don't know? How could you not know?" I asked, impatient with him and with my own curiosity.

"Eyes close," he admitted, not looking at me.

I couldn't tell if he was embarrassed by his lack of English or his squeamishness.

"Ask Pyro," he finally got out, as though that made everything clear.

"Pyro? Who's Pyro? I don't know Pyro."

"You do." He smiled like a man with a secret.

Pyro turned out to be Eddyberto, one of my brightest students. (I didn't want to know where the "Pyro" came from.) Aside from his usual school assignments, I'd seen a number of Eddyberto's drawings and knew that he was an extraordinary self-taught artist. He did remarkable pencil sketches, intricately composed and perfectly executed. All of his work had a dark, mythic quality to it, and his images often reflected his Aztec background.

I soon found out, however, that corrections saw a lot more in his artwork than I did.

One day after class Eddyberto showed me a drawing he'd done. The paper was crammed with mysterious images, some overlapping, others melting into each other. I liked it and hung it up on the bulletin board, until, that is, Sergeant Vallain came to see me with the drawing in his hand.

"You see this figure here, with the wide-brimmed hat?" the sergeant said, his voice trembling with excitement, his finger practically breaking through the paper he was poking it so hard. "That's El Senor. Kingpin, symbol of a drug lord.

"And this clown's face with the tear? That's no clown. Far from it. That's a gunrunner."

I'd been teaching in prison long enough to know not to argue with anybody from corrections. As civilians we'd had it drummed into us from all directions that we were guests in DOC's house and should act like it.

So I didn't say anything back to Sergeant Vallain even when it was obvious that the images he pointed out were all death heads in various guises. Actually, the whole piece was loaded with allusions to death and the afterlife, since the lesson I'd been teaching the day Eddyberto did the sketch was on the literary device of allusion.

It was soon after Sergeant Vallain confiscated Eddyberto's drawing that Edgar came to class with his freshly carved heart and told me that Eddyberto, aka Pyro, was the tattoo artist who did it.

"He's the best one in the place," Jacob and Ishmael jumped in. The two brothers, only two years apart, both lifted up the legs of their oranges to flash identical snake-entwined calves.

When I told Eddyberto what the other guys said about his skill, he didn't decline the honor.

And when I asked him how he managed to do such involved tattoos under jailhouse conditions, he wasn't reluctant to talk about it.

I had a hard time understanding him and following his description. His English was still pretty jagged and stumbling even though he'd come to the United States when he was a baby. And of course, his inherent suspiciousness of authority didn't help much.

From what I could figure out, it involved the motor taken out of a Walkman, a needle fashioned from a sharpened paper clip ("And where'd he get that, I wonder?" I could hear Sergeant Vallain asking), and chessmen or checkers melted down. Somehow he captured the smoke from the melted game pieces in a plastic bag, then mixed it with shampoo to make the ink!

I was queasy enough just listening to the murky details of the equipment he used that when he started talking about exactly how he etched the pigment into the skin I cut the lecture short.

Even so, I couldn't help but be awed by Eddyberto's gifts. The whole procedure sounded impossible, if not downright magical; the boy was an alchemist as well as an artist.

But DOC wasn't interested in whether Eddyberto was a magician or not. They had bigger and better things to nail him on.

Several weeks after Sergeant Vallain had taken Eddyberto's drawing and I'd learned about his skills, the sergeant appeared outside my classroom as the day was ending and waited while Officer DeLucia frisked the students.

"You'll be interested to know, sir," he said after everybody was out, in that forced courteous tone correctional staff was instructed to use in dealing with civilians, "that when I checked with the national gang database, the feds have listed this young man as a potential threat to national security, involved in all kinds of gang and potential terrorist activities.

"And now *we've* got him."

Obviously the lexicon of subversion had shifted significantly since September 11. Now a kid who drew pictures full of primitive and urban symbols, and who undoubtedly was a gang member—this in a society that mandated some sort of group affiliation in order to survive, whether it be church, a college fraternity, a political party, a country club, or a street gang—was suddenly a terrorist. Or perhaps it only confirmed the ancient belief that all artists were at heart insurgents.

Soon after that conversation with the sergeant, Eddyberto's Legal Aid lawyer told him that he'd be deported the day he was released from jail. Immigration Services would meet him at the gate, immediately drive him to Newark Airport, and send him back to Panama, a country he hadn't lived in past infancy, a country where he didn't have even a distant cousin, a country where no one but the authorities knew about him, where no one, not even those authorities, wanted him.

News like that flies fast around prisons, especially places like the Westchester County jail filled with dozens of illegals from Central America.

The guys in my class talked about nothing else, but never when Eddyberto was in the room. For weeks they analyzed and debated his situation the way they'd seen countless lawyers hack away at the facts. And everybody swore that their facts were right, even though they might contradict somebody else's.

But they all agreed on the injustice and illegality of it.

"The feds can't do something like that, throw somebody outta the country just 'cause he's Spanish, I mean, everybody's got their fuckin' rights," Swato, a self-styled suburban anarchist who worked hard to be anything but white, argued.

"Nay, dude, you got it all wrong, it's not the feds, it's friggin' Yonkers 5–0 behind it. They always be hatin' Pyro ever since he got that asshole Duggan in trouble for police brutality," Rosario said, born and bred in this country, but never very good in social studies.

"No, DOC, they get Pyro for cuttin' us. See?" Edgar pointed to his arm. It was the most words he had ever said in class at one time.

"You amigos don't know what the hell you're talking about," Officer DeLucia tried to derail them. "You just keep repeating all the crap you hear back on the block, then swear on your mother's underwear—no disrespect—that it's true. It ain't true just because you say it is. So let's cut all the jabbering and get some work done."

DeLucia was an older man, close to retirement at sixty-five, who usually didn't let much get to him—inmates or administration. He spent most of his days doing the daily crossword and calculating down to the penny what his pension would be on that long-awaited golden day. But he could see the panic in a lot of the young Latinos' eyes, black and wide with terror that the same thing could happen to them, and he had to show them some mercy.

But through all this, Eddyberto carried the fact of his exile with dignity. He carried it with the same dignity he carried his own tattoos, his knife scars, his native history, his gang pride, and his creative talent.

Now, though, he had something much more valuable than anything the other guys might contrive to carry with them, something more dangerous, more powerful, yet something official and sanctioned, given to him compliments of the feds: he was deemed a threat to national security.

Maybe that was why he became even more flagrant in his tattooing. He had nothing to lose now. Suddenly his artwork appeared all over the place: arms, necks, the back of hands. Even envelopes addressed to girlfriends, mothers, children; and the fabric canvases of county oranges were tagged with his designs.

"You know, once he'd found out about his getting deported he even stopped charging for his work," DeLucia told me after Eddy-berto was discharged and picked up by Immigration Services.

Maybe the only payment he needed was knowing that long after his exile, long after anyone would even remember his name, those men and boys he had tattooed would carry with them, wherever they went, and for as long as they lived, the pictures and patterns that he, Pyro, alchemist and artist, conjured up out of nothing but smoke and shampoo.

Chapter Eleven

Mothers of Invention

 M an on the block, ladies. Man on the block," Officer Collier bullhorned down the hallway.

"Look sharp."

Officer Collier was doing what she usually did: looking out for me two mornings a week as I made my way to my classroom on the women's unit, another shuffle in my teaching assignment.

She was a stolid woman in her late fifties who'd been working with the women for thirty years. Her presence was as dependable as the jail routine. Bible studies on Monday; linen change on Wednesday; outdoor rec on Fridays. The only thing unpredictable about Ms. Collier was her hair—short, brilloed, and Technicolor: Henna. Chrome yellow. Midnight black.

The women loved her hair, and they loved her, too.

Of course, they grumbled and growled and cursed (under their breath, "'cause Ms. Collier don't mess around") but they did what she asked, and played with her the way children might tease a stern parent but one they knew they could trust, something so few of them had ever had.

"Hey, Ms. Collier, how about black-and-white stripes," I'd heard Andrea, a skeleton of a white girl whom drugs had made unafraid of anybody—big or bad—quip one day.

"Man, on the block," Ms. Collier bellowed.

"Desiree, get back in there and put a T-shirt on under that top. You know the rules."

It was a difficult walk, that hallway, lined with cells, a steamy shower stall shielded by a windowed door, and two small phone booths.

I moved down that corridor like a monk in a brothel. I kept my eyes down so I'd only glimpse the bras and panties hanging on improvised clotheslines or the women's unmade beds with rumbled sheets that suggested an intimacy out of place there. They'd drape themselves in their cell doorways as though they had nothing else to do and try to catch my eye, despite Ms. Collier's commands to "move it along, ladies."

I didn't look up or take a relaxed breath until I was behind my classroom door.

But things weren't really that much more relaxed in the room. Ms. Collier's "man on the block" called for a decorum that most of my students couldn't maintain no matter how hard any of them tried.

Once I'd had the room set up, I'd give Ms. Collier the go-ahead. She'd call for school over the PA system, and the girls slouched into the room one by one. They didn't come in with the usual notebooks, pens, and pencils other kids brought to school. They couldn't. DOC had deemed it all contraband.

But that didn't mean the girls came in unencumbered.

The women's unit, more so than the men's jail, ran on an emotional dynamo fueled by jealousies and attachments, a dynamo that every once in a while exploded because everybody was into everybody else's business.

Like the time Smokey, who never missed a class, suddenly didn't show up for several days.

"Anybody know what's going on with Smokey?" I asked.

Dumb question.

Of course, they all knew what was going on with her.

"She beat the shit out of Krystal Star," Amber, a thimble-size fifteen-year-old that no group home could handle, spoke up.

"She's on lockdown, and can't come to school."

"But I thought they were best friends," I said, inadvertently stumbling into the gossip trap.

"Yeah, well, they, like, were, until Smokey found out that Krystal Star let that crackhead, Wibble, use the special lotion she bought for her," Amber filled me in as though we were both addicted to the same soap opera.

Of course, those weren't their real names.

Jail is a place where people reinvent themselves. Nobody is who they say they are, the same way nobody has done what they've been accused of doing.

So Amber was really Stacy, Smokey was Stephanie, Krystal Star, Tanisha. I didn't know about Wibble since she was an older woman with pipe cleaner limbs I'd only seen roaming the halls.

If I forgot and called one of them by her given name it was as though I'd insulted her or blurted out some family scandal in front of the whole class.

"I don't want people knowing my gov'ment name," they'd spit at me like a cobra fresh out of the basket.

I never understood what was behind that objection. They missed the central irony of their situation that since they were in jail their names were common chattel. As soon as they were booked, their names were broadcasted on everything from the plastic ID cards they had to carry to every criminal database in the country.

Still there was real poetry in the names they made up for each other. Those jailhouse tags captured who they were right there, right then, in that place.

Smokey was just that—laid-back, jazz club easy, illusive, but potentially acrid, and lethal if you got too much of her. And Krystal Star, a methamphetamine addict, was wild, bright, and funny, a nerve exposed, brittle as fine crystal.

Except for Ms. Collier, there wasn't much the girls paid attention to. As far as they were concerned, having a man on the block was just one more restriction that they ignored like no Walkmans after ten o'clock or no visits to another girl's cell.

The way they handled *this* man on the block was to pretend I wasn't there.

They didn't care that I was sitting right at the same table as they were. Some girl would still grind her heel into her latest honey's crotch who just happened to be sitting across from her with her legs wide open.

"Feet on the floor, ladies," I soon learned to intone throughout my morning, long past being self-conscious about it.

"Feet on the floor."

And it didn't matter to them that I heard them laughing hysterically about how Weather (everybody knew she was bipolar and sometimes refused to take her meds and so she was up and down like the weather) was always copping extra sheets off of Smitty, the mad fat and mad blind CO in charge of linen; or how you got a free phone call out of the reverends.

"Just get all weepy," Eppy (short for Episode, since, as she claimed, every day was a new episode in jail) would scoff at the ministers' kindness, "and they'll let you call any nigga you want."

But as much as they gossiped and talked and spilled everybody's secrets in front of the "man on the block," there was one thing they never talked about, and I wished they would.

Everybody knew that the men and women were always sending love letters to each other on the blocks, but no one knew how they did it. At least, none of the other civilians I asked. Of course, the COs would never tell us, if they knew, and I wasn't so sure they did.

DOC worked hard to make sure that the men and women didn't have any direct contact. The men were housed on the next floor down from the female unit. They never went to court together. They had separate clinics, separate church and bible study, separate rec areas. Even the elevator between floors had to be keyed by a CO.

Still there was this constant game of matchmaking. The girls in my class were always swapping names. Nacho gave Jasmine the name of her cousin, Hightop who was going upstate for ten years; or Birdy hooked up Tony, her brother or half brother or maybe not her brother at all, she just knew her mother raised him, with her latest girlfriend, Ladybug.

They were always trying to pull me into it.

"Mr. C, do you have Charlemagne in your men's class?" Eppy would ask.

"He's a big black dude, kinda dumb but real diesel," she'd barrel on, ignoring my obvious stonewalling look.

"How about Dwight?" RoseRose might jump in. "He's my cousin's cousin. He's like dumb thin, light skinned. He's got a gold tooth?"

I was always amazed how accurate they were. They knew exactly what guys were locked up, where they were housed, what their charges were, and what kind of time they were looking at.

One morning, though, Ayesha finally solved the mystery for me, at least part of it.

"Ayesha, you know school's not for sleeping," I said.

I was nagging her about nodding off in class.

"But, Mr. C, you don't understand," she whined. "I can't get no sleep. It's so noisy on the block with them shouting back and forth through the heating vents all night."

"Heating vents? Who's shouting?"

At times Ayesha could be pretty crazy. I wondered if this was one of those times. I'd have to check with Ms. Collier and find out if she was refusing her meds again.

"The vents, the ones that come up through the cells? All these dumb bitches yelling through the vents to the guys on the block downstairs," she tried to explain.

"The yelling's bad enough," she went on wide awake now, "but then them hos get pissed 'cause they hear some other bitch yellin' to some player they been writing to. Then the po-lice gotta be called, then we never get no sleep."

Heating vents! Alexander Graham Bell and Samuel Morris had nothing on these ladies for inventiveness.

The girls were furious with her for talking.

"Eh, Ayesha, shut up, you're crazy. You don't know what you're talking about.

"You're just jealous because that Mexican from Peekskill won't have nothing to do with you. And he hasn't even seen how ugly you are!" Gypsy goaded.

They all hated Ayesha. They were afraid of her dark moods and frenetic outbursts. They made fun of her pitch-black skin, mottled pink in places from a skin disease, and her bloodshot eyes, a side effect of her medication. She was the only inmate the other women hadn't bothered to nickname.

But then again, her own mother hadn't even bothered to name her.

When Kay, the school social worker, tried to help Ayesha get some kind of public assistance after she was released, she dug up a copy of Ayesha's birth certificate. The space for a first name was filled in as "Not Known." That left Ayesha officially nameless and in a legal limbo. "So what I do," she explained to Kay, "is every time I get sent to a different rehab or group home or jail I make up a new name for myself."

"He did too write," Ayesha sputtered like a red-hot coal.

"He wrote me three kites just yesterday."

All you had to do was see one of those letters to understand why they were called kites.

When inmates wanted to get letters to other inmates, they'd fold them up into the lopsided rectangular shape of a kite, put the names and blocks on the outsides, and drop them in a DOC "mailbox" for delivery.

The kids I taught were usually deeply suspicious of corrections. However, when it came to their letters to each other, they were remarkably trusting. They dropped those letters in the box as though all those folds and creases were padlocks that were guaranteed to keep corrections out of their business.

I was surprised by this Peter Pan faith in their right to privacy. DOC made it clear to everybody in the jail that all inmate communications were routinely looked at. Even the drawings and lettering they did on the outside of this strange jailhouse origami were scrutinized for gang symbols.

Still those letters sailed around the place like the lighthearted, carefree child's toys they were named after.

I knew DOC wouldn't distribute mail between the male and female units, so I never understood how they got those kites to each other.

Turned out that I wasn't going to find that out that day, either.

Eppy and Krystal Star had joined in on Gypsy's taunting and were working together like flint against steel to get Ayesha all fired up.

They all knew that despite Ayesha's initial "fuck you"s it was easy to reduce her to tears. The girls weren't like the guys I taught. If some kid was as pathetic as Ayesha they'd adopt and protect him. Not the women, they were cruel, and gratuitously so.

"The only kite he'd send you," Krystal baited, "would be to tell you to hang up."

"Don't be stupid, Star," Eppy shouted over the other girls' laughter in a mock talk-show hostess voice. "He wouldn't do *that*. He wouldn't want to waste the paper."

"Hey, Ayesha, better tell the nurse to up those Thorazine skittles they give you. You must be seeing things again," Gypsy finished off before Ms. Collier came in.

When the ladies were frothed for the kill like that, no amount of "That's enough! Get back to work" or "Stop it, now" worked.

On days like that, I just opened the door and Ms. Collier cleared the room.

But I didn't have to wait long for the final mystery of the kites to be solved.

Next morning, Anna put the last piece of the puzzle in place.

Anna was facing serious time with the feds. She'd been locked up already for over eighteen months while the lawyers haggled over her charges and sentencing. She'd been in jail so long she had a string of nicknames—Angel, Jelly Bean, Anna Banana, Candy. Most of the inmates who gave her those names were long gone.

She'd dropped out of school at fourteen, got kicked out of her parents' house at fifteen, and by seventeen had two brand-new cars, an apartment of her own, and an income that far exceeded her father's salary as a baker.

"I was good at what I did, Mr. C, I'm not gonna lie," she told me the first time we met. By then she had already gotten her GED with some of the highest marks possible.

"I was good with numbers and I had a lot of people working for me who knew I meant business," she explained, sounding like the tough, hard-nosed drug baroness that she was.

I'm sure the feds were glad to get her off the streets.

"Nobody wanted to cross me."

I could believe it.

Anna was a mountain of a young woman, solidly built but lithe in spite of her heft. She wore her auburn hair in a braid that went down to her waist. Her thick dark eyebrows and chestnut eyes made her smooth ivory skin even paler.

Anna wasn't like the other women. She didn't change how she looked. Her oranges were always clean and crisp and worn to regulation. She kept her hair in the same tightly plaited braid.

There was nothing about her that called attention to herself, and that was exactly what called attention to her. She was clearly a young woman who knew what she was about, who didn't flatter fashion by bowing to its whims. She said what she had to say. She'd just as soon compliment you as call you a piece of shit. I'd heard her do both.

Even though Anna was twenty-two and already had her GED, I still allowed her to come to class. She loved to learn and encouraged the other students to do what they had to do. She tutored in class; she tutored older women on the block; and she happily did extra work outside of school. Her plan was to get her BA and her MBA while in federal prison. She knew she'd have time on her hands.

"It's scary! I mean, I don't want to go back out to the way I was living, but it's going to be hard not to," she explained as she laid out her plans for the future as meticulously as the CPA she aspired to become.

"I mean, I never touched the stuff I was selling, but I'm addicted to all that money and all those people looking up to me. All that power. Even talking about it now, I get this rush."

She still had that kind of power in jail.

Everybody talked to her, and she knew everything that was going on. Even correctional staff let their guard down with her, seduced by her maturity and level-headedness. I was surprised one day to hear Ms. Collier, who was usually as forthcoming as Lot's wife after her fatal turn, telling Anna about problems her grandson was having on the streets.

The morning after Ayesha's outburst Anna was in class early to help me set the room up for the day.

"Mr. C, did you hear what happened to WildThing yesterday afternoon?"

Anna couldn't wait to tell me.

WildThing was really Heather, a firecracker of a girl. Whenever she came to class the whole room popped and crackled with energy, so I never knew which way she'd sway the group.

"I knew her grandmother," Ms. Collier warned me the first day Heather was scheduled to come to class.

"The poor woman hadda turn her out at twelve, even though she been taking care of her since she was four and her mother died from AIDS. But she had to. She had no choice. Heather was smoking dope and bringing men into her house for money.

"At twelve! Right in the woman's house!"

Since then Heather had been in and out of the system. At eighteen she'd already done state time. Nothing seemed to help, and nobody was optimistic, including Heather.

"She's in deep, deep shit...oops, sorry...this time," Anna rushed into her story.

"You know how the girls are always lowering their kites down to the men over the outdoor rec deck wall? Tying them up with yarn from socks," she said, finally enlightening me.

"Well, what some of those bitches do is tie their letters up in their panties and lower them down! You wouldn't believe it. Some of them even got guys sniffing their underwear then sending them back up with... well, you know."

Anna saw the look on my face and pushed on. She wasn't about to lose a chance to pass on some hot information.

"Anyways, WildThing's just plain stupid. She's always out there, screaming all this disgusting slut stuff to whatever guy she can. Everybody knows DOC's been watching her so when she's out there nobody'll go near the place.

"So, anyways, last night, she got caught pulling up a pair of panties stuffed with weed and pills.

"Ms. Collier was the one who called the code. She musta been watching her for a while. ERT took her down pretty bad. She'll be on lockdown forever now, and they're bringing outside charges against her.

"She's really screwed now." She sighed, shaking her head.

We both went about our business, caught up in our own thoughts. I wrote the day's assignments on the board. Anna turned on all the computers.

Anna obviously enjoyed telling me about last night's escapade. After all, gossip in jail was currency, and currency was power.

But I could tell that the sad waste of Heather's life hadn't escaped her, the same way the sad waste of her own life didn't go unnoticed.

There was a lot of waste in prison. Not the kind that Warden Morgan, the warden in charge of the female unit, harped about. He was a tall, lanky white man whose frowning walrus mustache was the only thing that gave his stone-set face expression. He harangued the officers about it and made the COs count out squares of toilet paper and ration tampons.

Nor was it the waste Warden Clooney ranted about in orientation, happily scandalizing the professionals by calling inmates "nothing but human garbage."

It was a different kind of waste.

You saw it every day in the county lockup.

Men and women, young and old, walking up and down those halls, some with an assured bounce to their step, others with the shuffle of defeat. Either way each one of them was a waste of abilities, dreams, and ambitions; of families, friendships, and decent human feelings.

And the waste wasn't limited just to inmates. I'd heard enough stories from different COs, stories of failed expectations, ravaged family lives, and crippling addictions to realize that those halls and blocks were as much a sump to their dreams as they were to the inmates'.

Then, as though she'd read my dark thoughts, Anna suddenly beamed up at me from the computer keyboard.

"We had the best party last night for Nile's birthday." She laughed.

I wasn't sure I wanted to hear about it. The young guys I taught were always getting locked down for their revelries because to them "party" meant black-market cigarettes, jailhouse hooch, and smuggled-in weed finished off with fights, stuffed up and overflowing toilets, and smoldering mattresses.

"I made her a great cake," Anna boasted.

I figured that hearing about Niles's party was a lot better than sitting with those ghosts of accumulated sadness, and so I gave her an encouraging smile.

"How does anybody make a cake in jail?" I asked, even though I was a little afraid of what I was going to hear—although it couldn't have been as bizarre and baroque as Eddyberto's description of his tattooing process from a year or so ago.

It turned out, however, that Anna was quite the caterer. Whenever any of the women had a birthday, or was being discharged, or just had had a good day in court, they all got together, pooled what food they had, and passed it onto Anna who would create some gourmet treat, by jail standards.

"Easy," Anna said, launching into her recipe with the eagerness of a suburban housewife.

"First, you take some cookies, crush 'em up real fine, then melt up some chocolate bars, mix it together with some milk, then you pour it into a plastic bowl, pat it down, and sprinkle the top with some kind of cereal, I like Cap'n Crunch myself. After that, all you got to do is pop it into the microwave."

"Oh, my God, Anna, my teeth hurt just hearing about it," I grimaced, feeling my jaw.

"Yeah, but Nile loved it." Anna grinned.

"I'm sure she did."

Nile was another eighteen-year-old who had had more time in juvenile detention and jail than school. With her swarthy parchment-like skin and silt-black hair, she looked as though she had just walked out of the Valley of the Kings.

"Has she come down from her sugar high, yet?" I laughed.

"Well, Ms. Tootle, the midnight CO? She had a hellava time getting her settled down for the night," Anna said.

"But the cake was fan-tastic."

"I'm still amazed that you can do that kind of thing in here."

"Oh, that's nothing," Anna went on, obviously pleased with herself.

"We make grilled cheese using the iron.

"And you've never tasted my banana pudding pie. That's what I'm most proud of. It's *my* recipe."

After the cake, I guardedly sucked a back molar.

"What you do is take cereal and crunch it up, then you mush up a couple of honey buns, and knead that all together."

Knead? Knead?

I was impressed. I was beginning to wonder if the ladies on the block had switched from the savagery of Jerry Springer to the domesticity of a cooking channel.

"Then you press it down around your bowl so it's like a crust."
Anna shaped her fingers to the contours of an imaginary bowl.

"You mash up a bunch of bananas, the riper the better, but that's
pretty easy in this place. DOC must get their bananas cheap 'cause
they're practically rotten. Then, you pour that into your crust, pop
it into the microwave for just about a minute, and you've got a nice
banana pudding pie."

I expected Anna to spread out a starched linen napkin in front
of me and serve up a healthy portion of her confection.

"*All* the girls want my pudding," she boasted. This time, though,
she wasn't the street entrepreneur, but the little kid on the playground with the latest toy.

Watching Anna put out books and supplies, a big smile warm-
ing her face, you'd never guess that her life was as bleak as it was.

But then, she hadn't survived her eighteen months in the county
lockup waiting for the feds to claim her by fretting over the power
of fate, or bad luck, or human frailty or human stupidity, or the
hand of God that put her there.

She just wouldn't give up or give in, the same way so many of
the other girls locked away with her—WildThing, Krystal Star,
Smokey, Ayesha—refused to surrender to the drag of society's millstone.

Some people would call that refusal denial; some would call it
resilience; others, sheer animal instinct. Whatever the label you put
on it, it all amounted to the same thing. They each fashioned and
reshaped the raw experience of their lives in order to get through
life, in order to *have* a life.

Anna, like most of the other girls in my class, knew that this
life, no matter how sad or lonely or bitter or empty or unfair, no
matter how fucked up or fucked over, *this* life was better than
no life at all.

So they did what they had to do. They wrote love letters to guys
they'd never see, or they bought a special hand lotion for a honey
they knew would cheat on them.

They made love with the heel of their foot, or twisted other people's kindness to get what they wanted.

They sold their dirty underwear for a fistful of drugs, or they popped a banana pudding pie into the microwave and hoped it would come out okay.

They knew that things would get better. They had to.

Chapter Twelve

Word

They all knew where words could get you.

After all, half the inmates were locked up for mouthing off at the cops.

"Them assholes think they can pull you in for any shit they want," Lincoln, as tall and chiseled faced as his namesake, complained.

It was the third time in the past six months that he had gotten himself arrested for telling a cop to go fuck himself.

"I was just demanding my rights," he explained.

So what if the car was stolen? He didn't know it.

And the drugs? They weren't his.

"I told the po-lice that, but they don't wanna hear it. They're just a bunch of stupid motherfuckers, always trying to fuck you over," he protested.

This time, however, he didn't just tell it to the cops.

He told it to the judge, and the judge didn't waste any words.

"One year in the county pen."

If the men knew *where* words could get you, they also had their own ideas about *what* words could get you—money, fame, cars, jewelry, notoriety, and the babes. That's why every block had at least three or four rappers who swore they were about to make it big.

I could always tell which of my students had aspirations. Their heads bopped, their lips spit out beats, their hands flew across the penciled page carefully cropping and harvesting words; the whole thing—head, lips, hand, words—orchestrated and synchronized.

Those future hip-hop stars, though, couldn't be bothered writing a school essay, or doing a vocabulary assignment. Yo, man, they didn't have time. They had rhymes to write.

Some of them didn't even hear me when I'd stand over them and nag them to get some work done. I couldn't break the spell. They were as rapt and dazed as the ancients stumbling down from the caves of Mount Parnassus.

It was the same with the jailhouse poets, although they rightly suspected that there wasn't any money in poems. That didn't stop them from checking out the job prospects.

"How much you think I can make on a book of poems, Mr. C?" Kahlil, that crazy and dark poet, would ask. It was hard to imagine anybody wanting to read those notebooks filled with rhyming pain and paranoid visions.

"Not much, Kahlil, maybe even nothing," I'd deliver the bad news each time he asked.

"Well, what about that Raven guy, Poe? And Tupac?" Kahlil whined.

"They're both dead, Kahlil, died young at that."

Kahlil didn't give up easily.

"I mean, like if I got a bunch of my poems together and like sent them to a publisher, how much you think I get?"

Luckily there were other compensations for the efforts of poets like Kahlil.

Aside from that age-old currency of praise, the other inmates would offer to buy particular poems, especially love poems.

"Yo, man, that's deep. Can I get a copy of that for my shorties? I'll give you one soup for two poems," somebody like Jocko might bargain after hearing one of Kahlil's pieces. Jocko was a seventeen-year-old who could barely write his name and count past ten; still he prided himself on being a player who kept two or three girls going at once.

Poems circulated around the jail like dissident tracts in the old Soviet Union. I often wondered how many of the rhymes I'd been asked to read during my own long bid in the county jail were really just retreads from former bards in captivity. Who knows? Some of those love poems may have been in the jailhouse literary pipeline since its 1914 work farm days. After all, broken hearts, rampant lust, and boundless love are all pretty timeless.

Although the guys who bought those poems might be clumsy with words, they weren't stupid. They knew enough to copy them over in their own tenuous handwriting, all the while mumbling to themselves that their girl was going to love this.

The guys might not be stupid, but I was sure the women who got those poems weren't either. They must have known that their locked-up boyfriends didn't make them up. Maybe they just found it touching to think of them hunched over lined paper, painstakingly copying out the words, crumbling up sheet after sheet, trying to get it just right. For them!

The jailhouse poets weren't the only ones who turned a profit from their words.

Most of the men had a profound belief that if they made just the right combination of words they could convince the judge that they didn't do what they were accused of doing, that they were just in the wrong place at the wrong time with the wrong people.

And they were sure that if they sent enough letters to the court they wouldn't have to do state time, or do back-to-back bullets—sixteen months straight! And that's without blowing good time—or miss another Christmas with their son or daughter, or have another birthday locked up.

So, they hired some dude smarter than them for beef jerky or rice and beans, and they had him write a letter to the court filled with big words and promises. It didn't matter if the words weren't their own. The judge would never know the difference.

"Bullshit for a price," Eddie Rodriguez, one of those jailhouse scribes, called it.

But Eddie wrote those letters for nothing.

He was a lean, light-complected seventeen-year-old Puerto Rican. However, the only thing "Rican" about him was his name—

Eduardo Xavier Gomez-Rodriguez. Eddie had to work hard at being bad, at gettin' down with the brothers, words that sounded as foreign coming out of his mouth as the Spanish he barely knew, yet felt he should try to use.

He had to remember to yank his pants *down* his butt, not pull them up; to slouch and shuffle when he walked; to curse. And he had to work at *not* calling out the answers in class or getting interested in a lesson.

He had grown up in the rich suburb of Scarsdale and had almost gotten his high school diploma, until, as he put it, he got caught up in things. Eddie made sure nobody knew about the Scarsdale part or his near successes in school, the way nobody knew that his father was a hotshot Manhattan lawyer, the way nobody knew, including his father, where his mother disappeared to when Eddie was six.

What everybody did know was that from then on Eddie was always in trouble. He argued against every conceivable rule; and if he couldn't argue his way around it, or through it, he just bucked it.

At the same time he didn't seem to be having much fun. When he was younger it was as though he was being bad in order to force his mother out of hiding and straighten him out.

After a while, when that didn't happen, he seemed to lose the point of all that defiance and ended up breaking the law because it was there.

Up until now he had always been able to talk himself out of doing serious time. If that didn't work, his father's words usually did the trick.

Not this time.

Now he was sitting in the county pen, waiting for the bus to take him upstate for a five-year stretch after a series of armed robberies.

The other guys knew that Eddie loved to write and knew a lot of fancy words. They liked that when he wrote you a letter for the judge it was *your* letter. He didn't use a boilerplate for the court the way some of the other jailhouse scribes did, just changing the name, the dates, and the charge.

What really impressed them was that before he wrote anything, he'd sit you down and talk to you. He'd get a table in the dayroom far from the TV and ask you questions about yourself, about your life, your case. Not only that, he actually listened to what you said.

"So now tell me, how many bids have you done previously . . . I mean, before now?" he'd ask, leaning in close to his client like every lawyer he'd ever been bailed out by.

That's why the guys lined up to have Eddie do letters for them, and they practically pleaded with him to take something for his labors, a soup or a jar of peanut butter, anything.

"I'm good, man, I'm good," he'd explain, graciously blowing off their offers. "I just like fuckin' with the system."

Aside from the raps and the poems and the letters, there were certain words that could stand all on their own, words like *Bloods, Crips, Latin Kings.* They had their own cachet, their own power like talismans snuck in from the outside world.

The men plastered these gang tags all over the place along with other, less familiar names—NewRock, Bay Street, Bowman Towers—more neighborhood posses than gangs, really just bunches of boys hanging together because you need to hang with somebody, and you might as well call yourselves something.

The guys were pretty bold about it, decorating their schoolwork with them, or their books and folders, scratching the names into the tables they worked on.

They were pretty bold about it until, that is, DOC did a security sweep checking for gang graffiti. Then word would get out that ERT, the emergency response team, was on a tear searching the blocks and the classroom, and suddenly they'd start furiously erasing their folders, frantically tearing out pages from their notebooks, and scrambling to sit at a different desk.

However, it wasn't always gang stuff.

The guys embellished their letters and envelopes with other, even more powerful words—the names of their latest girlfriends, or of their babies, or of their babies' mamas, or even of their own mamas. And some, like Ray from years ago on his twenty-first birthday, preached the more universal sentiments of peace, one love, and freedom.

The inmates weren't just greedy for the words themselves, though. They were greedy for the things that made them.

Everybody bugged me for paper and pens. Even older inmates, men I didn't know, begged for writing paper, their manners impeccable.

"'Cuse me, Teach, awful sorry to bother. You happen to have any extra paper I could have?" some bristle-faced man would stick his head into my classroom and ask.

Pens were as coveted as nickel bags.

The only pens inmates were allowed to have were the ones they could buy through commissary since regular pens were contraband.

When I handed out ballpoints for the GED essay or any of the state-mandated tests, I had to count them out and count them back in like a nurse handling controlled substances.

At first I didn't understand their hunger for those pens, until I saw one of the guys trying to write with one from commissary. It was like the inside of a BIC without the plastic case, a wiggly worm of tubing about as long as a pinkie finger. When you tried to write with it, it collapsed in your hand or slipped out of your fingers. They certainly couldn't be used as weapons since they could hardly be used as pens.

But as much as those jailhouse rappers, poets, lovelorn boyfriends, courthouse scribes, and graffiti artists knew about the power of words, they still weren't convinced about the value of books or interested in reading them.

There were, of course, the guys who only read urban lit. They were happy to have reflected back to them, page after page, everything they already knew about themselves, or every homeboy they ever hung out with, or every crackhead they ever sold to, or every bitch they ever fucked. The sex, the violence, and the drugs were the only things that legitimized a book in their eyes.

Although it didn't happen often, there occasionally were a few guys who weren't afraid to go into literature's unfamiliar territory.

Dario had always loved books despite a childhood of homeless shelters, foster parents, and group homes. A veteran of the county and state penal system, he still loved books.

"You got any books I could read?" he asked shyly the first time that I met him when, at sixteen, he came into my classroom.

"You know, real books, not like the stuff some guys get into," he whispered, not wanting to offend anybody.

That wouldn't be the only time Dario would ask me for books. Over the next several years as he came in and out of jail, in and out of the special housing unit for the worse troublemakers according to DOC, he'd read his way through whatever books I gave him.

"I wasn't like the other kids," he told me. "When the social workers came in the van to drag me off to the next group home or detention center—I was bad even back then, so I was always getting kicked out of somewhere—I didn't worry about keeping my clothes together or junk like that.

"Me? I'd be stuffing some dirty old pillowcase full of my favorite books, the ones I'd been lugging around for years, like my beat up *Doctor Dolittle*, *The Hobbit*, a few Oz books. You know, the ones I'd been reading, like, forever. Even when I ran away from wherever I was I always had my books."

It was pretty hard to imagine him at six feet two inches with his glossy, coal-black skin and pumped muscles as that innocent little boy carting around a sackful of books.

He didn't remember how he got to be so interested in reading. He just always was.

"I mean, as far back as I can remember, there was a book," he puzzled with me on more than one occasion.

"I don't know. Knowing me, I probably stole that first one." He laughed at his own expense.

"I mean, I grew up in shelters, and there were always books around, you know, the beat-up kind other people's kids don't want anymore. So I probably just ripped it off, thinking I was putting it over on somebody.

"Whatever. I just got hooked." He shook his head ruefully like an addict confessing to his obsession.

Wherever his love of reading came from it was more than credible. Dario would be the only student I had in jail who'd be finishing up high school with honors.

Jimmy was another lifelong reader who bragged to me that he had actually been sitting in a reading group at his local library when the cops came to arrest him this last time.

"It was kinda weird. I was sitting in this big leather chair in the library reading room with a bunch of ladies. It's a great place with all this dark wood and these old paintings of guys who'd been dead a hundred years.

"Me and the ladies were talking about *Fried Green Tomatoes* when these two Yonkers cops showed up in the doorway.

"I don't know if you've ever seen Yonkers 5–0 but they're not a pretty sight. For once they didn't come in swinging, which is their usual MO. They just stood there, looking at me, and let me finish what I was saying about Evelyn Couch and Mrs. Threadgoode being friends.

"I knew why they were there, and I knew enough not to push my luck. So as soon as I was done, I asked the ladies to excuse me and walked out into the hall.

"The ladies'll be wondering what happened to me," he said as he ransacked my bookshelves for something he hadn't read, which was getting harder and harder.

"You got anything else by Dumas? I really liked *The Man in the Iron Mask*."

He was lucky to have had a third-grade teacher, Mrs. Bristle, who turned him into a reader.

"I even remember the book. *Stuart Little*. You ever read it? The one about the mouse, and him having a *real* family."

That was the last of Jimmy's luck.

His father was a Hell's Angel. When Jimmy was in the fourth grade his dad was killed in a motorcycle accident speeding down I-95 to Florida. He was clocked at one hundred miles an hour when a semi cut him off.

Word had it, though, that the accident was no accident. It was retaliation for a big drug deal that had crossed too many lines.

Then, a year after the crash, Jimmy's mom died of breast cancer, and he lived with a series of aunts and uncles who squabbled over the little money left in his mother's bank account.

Through it all he kept reading.

That's when he discovered libraries.

Even though he was shuffled from town to town depending on what relative needed his money the most, he always made sure to get a library card.

"A couple of months before the cops nabbed me, I was delivering pizza to the projects.

"Truth was, I was delivering a whole lot more than that, but my boss didn't know. He just liked the fact I'd go into neighborhoods his other drivers refused to.

"Anyway, in between runs, I'd do these quick trips into the library to pick up something to read.

"One day this librarian, Mrs. Dostal, I think that was her name, she was a nice lady, told me I should try their reading group.

"At first I didn't know what she was talking about. I mean, I liked to read; you finish one book, you start another, right? I didn't know people sat around and talked about them!"

He got the hang of it after the first meeting.

Plus the ladies loved him...

Besides inheriting a little bit of cash and his father's two mint-condition Harley classics, which were sitting in his uncle Jake's garage (the only relative he trusted), Jimmy also inherited his father's blond hair, intense blue eyes, and charm with women.

"They really got off on having this young dude talking books with them." He smiled mischievously, as if they had done a lot more with him than discuss plot and character development in the latest Oprah pick.

As much as guys like Jimmy and Dario loved books and had a profound faith in the words that made them, I couldn't get away from the fact that that obviously wasn't enough to keep them out of prison.

Still, I wanted to believe that their passion for books would ultimately—somehow—make a difference in their lives.

I do know that I felt better seeing a student absorbed in a solid page of print instead of pawing over one of those soft-core porn magazines, the ones that disguise themselves as hot-rod magazines with half-naked women bent over the front fender checking the oil.

I certainly liked being asked my opinion about a particular novel or writer more than listening to complaints about how long a book was; or how boring one was that I had recommended; or answering for the thousandth time, to nobody's satisfaction, that most daunting question of all, "Why do we have to read stuff like this?"

Maybe it was just my own faint hope in a fairly hopeless world that at least while a kid was engrossed in a book, he was safe from the world of bars and slamming gates, of fights and lies, of watching your back and protecting what's yours; that, for that short time, he got to live in a world far different from his own.

Better yet, maybe there'd be a day when that same kid would suddenly recognize that the heart that beat in all the struggling characters he'd ever read and cared about was the same heart that beat in the judge who sentenced him, or the CO who harassed him, or the inmate who was begging to have the shit beat out of him.

And maybe, just that once, it would stop his tongue, hold back his fist.

Chapter Thirteen

Man-child

Warren had a problem.

He just wasn't the man he kept saying he was.

He was only a kid, a young, just turned fifteen-year-old kid at that, locked up in the county pen.

It didn't help that he was short and scrawny and had only five or six strands of wiry black hair reluctantly growing out of a soft chin.

He could certainly curse like a man, but the high-pitched croak that broke through when he got really mad or really excited drained off whatever testosterone he was able to muster and left the other guys laughing and him fuming.

He had his waves, of course.

He cultivated those concentric circles of nappy hair that rippled out from the crown of his head the way he did his chin beard. He spent hours brushing his hair in careful calculated strokes, always down and out from the center.

He brushed in my jailhouse classroom (where he wasn't supposed to), he brushed walking in the halls (where he wasn't supposed to), he brushed in church (where the ministers didn't care). At night he slept in his do-rag the way women in the old days slept in their hairnets.

There wasn't much the other guys envied Warren for, but they all coveted those waves.

"Hey, Warren, like those tsunamis," was a guaranteed way to get him to smile, something he hated to do since his baby-toothed grin made him look like the ten-year-old he almost still was.

And try being a man when you've got COs like Ms. Collier from over on the women's unit telling everybody how they knew you before you were born, how your mother had you while she was locked up, right there, across the rec yard, in the women's jail.

"She wasn't nothing but a little tick of a girl," Ms. Collier told me every time she came over to the men's unit to get some over-time.

"LyWanda was her name. Even pregnant she was small, so you couldn't tell she was carrying unless you knew.

"I'm not sure his mama was even sixteen when she first came in, but she was wild as a banshee," she said, wagging her hennaed head as though she still couldn't believe what she'd seen those fifteen years before.

"She was loud and scrappy and would take anybody on. Luckily for her, the other girls liked her and treated her like a doll."

I'd never met Warren's mother, and he never talked about her.

I did, however, meet Miss Montgomery, his grandmother, at one of our parents' nights. By then she was the one taking care of him, or trying to, at least.

Seeing her, it was easy to imagine that her daughter had been birdlike, loud, and a fighter.

Warren's grandmother was as thin as the wooden cane she walked with. She waved that thing in his face, drowning out his "Yes, ma'am"s as she lectured him about being good, going to school, and staying out of trouble.

"And what about church, child? Are you going to church?"

She complained about everything from the long bus ride to get there, to the lack of herbal tea and the long speeches those war-dens and preachers made taking up her time with her precious little boy.

"When LyWanda came in she just reeked of booze, the kind of soaked-in smell you get off the real alkies." Ms. Collier sighed with regret.

"I'm sure her being locked up saved that boy. Otherwise she

would've kept on drinking, and who knows what that boy would've come out like then."

As it was, the damage was extensive.

The alcohol had pretty much short-circuited Warren's body and brain, the same way Jason, long gone now to state prison, had had his chances in life destroyed by his mom's drug use. Warren's school records showed an IQ of seventy. He may have insisted that he was a man and could do anything he wanted, but that insistence couldn't make him read or do math or sit still long enough to let anything sink in.

That's why I was surprised when one day as I was handing out books with the faint hope that the guys would take them and read them on the block, Warren came up and asked for one.

"Whatta you got that's interesting, Teach? You got that book, *The Prince?*" Warren asked with his best swagger.

"Yo, Warren, you going to read it in the original I-talian?" Brandice said, a nineteen-year-old who had just gotten his GED and was feeling pretty cocky.

"Yeah, Brandy, the same way you're reading *The Art of War* in the original Chinese," Frankie shot back, getting the laugh he was looking for—which shut Brandice up.

Frankie was Warren's self-appointed guardian. He was one of the few white kids that nobody messed with. He was big and beefy, with a lot more muscle than anyone wanted to take on unless they had a reason, and Warren wasn't one of those reasons.

Machiavelli's *The Prince* and *The Art of War* by Sun Tzu were best sellers in the jail. Several tattered copies circulated from block to block and floor to floor.

I'm not sure anyone really read those treatises on deception and aggression, but the men, young and old, endlessly discussed how to use their tactics to get over on DOC.

I had no idea where those books came from originally, but it wasn't from my library. I refused to stock them. There was enough manipulation in the place.

But my students didn't want to hear that. As far as they were concerned I just didn't get it. That didn't stop them, though, from badgering me for them.

"Sorry, Warren, no *Prince* and no *Art of War*," I answered.

Usually when I started handing out books, Warren quietly slipped out of class. It was an arrangement we'd come to without talking about because we both knew that anything I had that was on his reading level would have compromised his already fragile manhood.

"How about *True to the Game?*" Warren persisted.

For some reason he was keeping himself on the frontlines.

True to the Game was another of one those books the guys hounded me for, that and anything by Sister Souljah or Donald Goines, books that seemed to celebrate the grit and sordidness of urban life and death.

"You know, Mr. C, there's a lot of irony in those books," Dario, my one reader of good *and* bad literature in that class tried to argue with me, sounding a bit ironic himself.

"Plus there are plenty of lessons, you know, the kind you're always saying we should look for."

"Such as?" I asked skeptically.

"Like that the drug trade is deadly, for one," he answered. "That family is more important than friends."

Dario may have been right. He was enough of a critical reader to be able to ferret out an author's intent, if there was any, that is, other than money.

But he was an army of one. No one else that I taught would get the point, or even think to look further than the curses and obscenities, the blood, the bodies, the booty that peppered those pages like random gunshots.

So, those titles weren't on my shelves either.

Of course the guys complained that my books were played, tired, stupid, lame, all synonyms for boring, which was a synonym for "too white" even if some of the authors—Richard Wright, Maya

Angelou, James Baldwin—were as black and poor as they were. Go figure.

Warren shuffled through the pile of books I had on the table.

"I seen the movie," he said, rejecting *The Outsiders.*

He did the same thing with *A Raisin in the Sun.* "The title's stupid."

The Contender: "But it's about boxing."

Durango Street: "Why's it got to be about a gang? Like, all kids are in gangs?"

There was no winning with Warren.

He grumbled that a book was about white people, or that it was about black people, or that it was too big, or the print was too small, or that it was a girl book, or that it was about sports, or not about sports.

"Don't you got anything about Tupac?" Warren whined.

But we both knew what he really was discontented about.

All the books were too hard for him to read.

"What about this one, Mr. C?" Warren asked, holding up a copy of *Of Mice and Men* in a last-ditch effort to leave the room with a book like everybody else.

"I heard about this book. My man, Roger, read it when he was locked up in Comstock."

"That's a good one, Warren," Brandice piped in again.

"You'd like it. There's this guy in there, his name's Lennie, actually he kinda reminds me of you, he's like..."

Brandice stopped. He wasn't stupid and read my stare right.

I knew where he was going.

Frankie did, too.

"Hey, Warren, this is a good one. I read it when I was locked down after that big fight on A block and had nothing else to do. Mr. C brought it to me," he said, tossing him a copy of *Manchild in the Promised Land.*

"It's this true story about this dude named Claude and him growing up in Harlem back in the day, and all the shit he gets into.

"I mean, this dude does all this crazy stuff, the kinda stuff me and my buddies used to do when we was kids." His eyes widened with excitement. I could just see him remembering all those pranks they'd pulled off.

"It's weird seeing that stuff in a book," he said.

He shook his head in amazement at what you can find on the printed page.

Warren was already picking his way through the book's first few sentences, his lips moving slowly from word to word.

"I think I'll take this one, Mr. C," Warren said.

He looked up at me with a big grin on his usually sullen face.

"I can take it back to the block with me, right?"

I never expected to see that copy of *Manchild in the Promised Land* again.

I figured he'd quickly lose interest once he'd struggled through enough words he couldn't decipher. Then it would get swallowed up in the usual maelstrom of the block until it was tossed out by ERT when they did one of their random sweeps, flipping mattresses, confiscating things they claimed were contraband, throwing things away for the sheer power of it.

But Warren brought it back to class the next day.

"I know I got math and stuff to do," he said once he settled down to his table, "but do you think I could read my book after I do my other assignments? I really like it."

"Well, I suppose," I said, struggling not to sound pleased.

"This guy is bad," he said as an afterthought, delivering the ultimate jailhouse compliment.

That was his routine for the next few weeks.

He did his other assignments as best he could. He copied a few, stuck a few into the back of other people's folders, tossed a few into the wastebasket when he thought I or Officer Ramos wasn't looking. Then he'd clear his desk, pull his chair up close to the table, and open the paperback to where he left off.

Warren was a careful reader.

He placed a paper straightedge under the line he was reading to guide his eyes. Then he'd pick his way across the page with his finger.

Sometimes he read the words softly to himself.

He laughed.

He sucked his teeth.

He snorted out a word of advice.

"That was stupid. Why'd you do that?"

Other times he'd get so excited he'd insist on reading to me. Then he'd pull out a chair next to him for me to sit down, and in a low confessional tone he'd parcel the words out to me.

The first time Warren went public with his reading I was ready for the worst.

He was pretty nasty a lot of the time and made enemies easily. Brandice wasn't the only one in class who wanted to see him get his, and Warren sounding stupid would've fit the bill perfectly.

For some reason, though, it didn't happen.

As he quietly whispered the words out from the page, the whole room held its breath. We were all pretty awed by what we were seeing, including Warren.

At times watching him struggle his way through *Manchild*, I wished that Warren could approach his life with as much care and attention as he did his reading.

Things would've been a lot easier for him if he had had the same kind of straightedge to guide the decisions he made, something that kept him on track and out of trouble, so that he didn't curse, didn't damn well brush his hair whenever and wherever he wanted, didn't let the other guys goad him into fighting over stupid stuff, didn't spend weeks in lockdown.

But that was asking too much.

The kid was reading a book and loving it.

At least for the hours he was reading, he was staying out of trouble. He might've been running from the cops down some Harlem alley, or beating the crap out of some guy, or selling drugs on some street corner, but at least for the moment it was somebody else's escape, somebody else's fight, somebody else's deal, while he was safe in the pages of his book.

Manchild's world was an easy one for him to inhabit. It was filled with everything he knew. Young bitches. Prostitutes. Guns. Gangs. Family conflicts. Friends on smack or dead in the streets. Kids like him in detention centers, jails, even Sing Sing, all places he'd been in himself or knew about from his boys, his uncles, or his cousins.

But at the same time he heard adults encouraging guys like Claude, guys like himself, adults who believed that young, troubled, black kids could make it out of the hood, that they could do something positive.

Better yet, he heard Claude agreeing with them, thinking it over, taking it seriously, not blowing it away as just some cracker social worker–type gassing him up.

It may have been an easy world for him to inhabit, but he didn't always like what happened in it.

One day, toward the end of the book, he came to class looking for a fight.

"Fuck this shit," Warren slammed through the door and threw his book across the table toward me.

"Hey, papi, you know you can't come in here cursing like that," Officer Ramos warned.

"I can do anything I want," Warren said, and walked over to the cabinet to get his work.

I could see where the morning was going.

"Come on, Warren, settle down," I jumped in before he and Ramos had the faceoff Warren was spoiling for.

"You know Ramos is just trying to keep you out of lockdown."

Warren didn't acknowledge me.

"Yo, my man, what's with you this morning?" Frankie tried, moving over to Warren's table.

"You okay?"

When Warren wouldn't even look up from the simple division worksheet he was pretending to do, Frankie just shrugged.

"Suit yourself, bro."

I didn't find out what was going on until after class.

"Warren, you didn't read your book today," I said, looking over the few math problems he did.

"I'm not reading it no more," he said, sounding like a little boy with hurt feelings.

"How come?"

Warren shrugged.

"I thought you liked the book. I mean you're almost finished."

"That was before he got stupid."

I'd worked with Warren long enough to know that it takes him a while to get to the point. The world moves pretty fast for people like him. Most people's lights have come on and gone off before Warren has even found the switch.

I shuffled the papers in his folder, wrote a comment on a three-sentence paragraph I'd already read once before, and waited.

"I don't get why he dumped Judy. She was the best girl he'd ever had. Why didn't he stay with her?" he said, as though he was the one who had been jilted.

"I mean, he'd had all those other bitches before her. But they weren't nothing like Judy. She was crazy about him, all the white girls were, but she was different. He says so. They don't even fuck for a long time. Sorry, Mr. C, but they don't. It says right in the book. But even after he gets some, he still dumps her."

Somewhere in Warren's puzzling out the pages he had missed the point.

It's Judy, white and Jewish, who leaves Claude despite their attraction to each other. When he doesn't hear from her in a while Claude makes a desperate effort to contact her, but her parents tell him she was sent away and that he'd never see her again.

Maybe that much prejudice and pain was as incomprehensible to Warren as the words on a page sometimes were.

Or, more likely, he knew only too well what that kind of rejection and disappointment felt like and couldn't face it, or let Claude face it.

So Warren had Claude do what he himself always did. He struck out and cut people off before they got to do it to him. Then, in a typical Warren move, he got mad at Claude for disappointing him and was ready to walk away from him.

I suspected I was one more disappointment to Warren, the way he glared at me across the table. I'd tricked him into reading a book only to have it turn out bad like everything else in his life.

"Of course, if you don't finish the book, you'll never know what happens. I mean, maybe Judy will come back?"

It was a cheap shot.

I knew Judy didn't come back. But I also knew that by the end of the story Claude realized that the streets weren't as powerful a center of gravity as he thought they were.

I didn't want Warren to miss that part.

Eventually, he finished the book.

And at his instigation we had a book party.

"Com'on, Mr. C, I mean, I never read a whole book before, ever, in my whole friggin' life," he pleaded.

Warren got his party.

It was over doughnuts and hot chocolate that I suggested he write a letter to Claude Brown.

"That's a stupid idea," Warren spit out.

"Thanks, Warren," I answered and pretended to reach across the table and take his cup of hot chocolate.

"No offense, Mr. C, but it is." Warren grinned, a mustache of powdered sugar on his upper lip.

"Claude Brown don't know me from squat. Besides, I wouldn't know what to say."

"All you have to do is tell him what you thought of the book. You could even ask him about Judy," I coaxed.

It took a while but Warren wrote his letter.

It was brief and to the point—well, to Warren's point.

He told Brown that he was locked up, that he read his book, that he liked it, but that he thought he was dumb for walking out on Judy.

"Who knows, maybe he'll write back," I said, handing it back to him.

As soon as I said it I saw my mistake. I knew I had just guaranteed that Warren would never send that letter.

If there was even the slimmest possibility that Claude might answer him, Warren wasn't going to take the chance that he wouldn't.

Claude had let him down once already when he dumped Judy.

Warren wasn't about to give him the opportunity to disappoint him a second time.

"Fat chance that'll happen," he snorted. "Fat chance."

And Warren stuffed the letter deep into the pocket of his county oranges.

Chapter Fourteen

Chicks in the Big House

Quick, quick! I think one's coming."

It was spring hatching time so I wasn't surprised to see the dim yellow light in the corner of the jail classroom. I was surprised, though, to hear Jonathan calling out from the incubator, his voice edgy as a midwife on her first case.

All my other students were busy doing their morning work details as part of a new program DOC was trying out with the help of a state grant. It was designed to help kids not come back to jail by giving them some counseling and job training while they were locked up, and I was lucky to have been assigned to it for a while. They did things their mamas probably would've dropped dead seeing them do. They scrubbed toilets, mopped floors, wiped down tabletops. They worked hard to deprive the cockroaches of a foothold, and they were proud of the fact that the dirt and smell of the rest of the jail—a cocktail of urine, sweat, semen, and dirty clothes—stopped at the gate of their block.

But Jonathan didn't care. He didn't care about anything.

He didn't care about doing his detail, and he didn't care about the demerit he'd get for his neglect.

I'd heard him say it enough times to believe him.

But he did care about those eggs slowly coming to life over the past twenty-eight days.

That's why he was there, in the dark, roosting.

Even after my eyes adjusted, I could barely make him out.

I've always thought of Jonathan as a chestnut. His skin has that deep, smooth, glossy brown of a newly opened husk. But it wasn't just his complexion that reminded me of a chestnut. Most days he was more like the fruit just dropped from the tree with its sharp spines. Those days nothing and nobody could get at him. Those days I wondered if anyone, anywhere had ever gotten to that shiny, tender core he so fiercely defended.

But that first morning, when the brood began to hatch, I didn't wonder. He was as tender as the eggs he guarded.

"One's coming, Mr. C, Number fourteen. It's rocking, and there's a little crack along the side," Jonathan whispered, as though it were a matter of soothing and not struggle that would hatch that chick.

He was sitting close to the incubator, all folded up, waiting.

Jonathan was a tall, pole-thin sixteen-year-old Dominican, whose shaved head, required by the youthful offenders program, made him look even taller.

He stared down through the glass top, his elbows resting on his knees as he sucked his thumb.

Jonathan wasn't like some of the other thumb suckers I'd had over the years. He didn't secretly slip it into his mouth, say, when the lights were dimmed for the Friday video.

He didn't hide it. Everybody just accepted the fact.

He had his own etiquette about it, though. He was careful not to shake hands if he'd been sucking his thumb, or to pass out papers.

He wasn't ashamed of it, but he did try to stop. Those days he'd wrap his thumb in a thick barrier of tape, swearing to everybody that this was IT, then he'd mope through his day.

"They almost cut it off when I was on Rikers Island in the city last time," he explained to me when I first met him.

"Everybody was some kinda gang member even if you didn't wanna be.

"It was the only way you could survive. So I got recruited by the Bloods, had all the fights, got the tattoo. It was okay for a minute, but after a while I didn't like some of the stuff I was suppose to do, like cutting up other DRs, so I told 'em I wanted out. That's when they threatened to cut my thumb off.

"It got crazy, what with all the fights and everything. I always had a coupla toothbrush shanks on me. I didn't go to school, didn't take a shower for a couple of weeks. Even scraped off the tattoo with a plastic spoon I sharpened up."

That explained the thick welt of scarred skin on Jonathan's upper arm.

"But it was worth it. I didn't wanna have anything to do with people who wanna cut somebody's thumb off," he said, the outrage in his voice making it sound like infanticide.

That morning, standing over Jonathan, I could hear a slight thumb-sucking sound and the plaintive peep of the struggling chick.

I took the lid off the incubator.

"Can you hear it? Put your ear closer. When it's time for them to hatch they start calling to each other, encouraging each other," I explained into Jonathan's wide-eyed stare.

"Yeah, yeah, I can," he answered, his thumb out of his mouth, both hands gripping the sides of the hot box. "And I think I hear something coming out of number seven, too."

When we first got the eggs, he helped write the numbers on them in blue marker. The numbers were the only way we could keep track of the required twice daily turning. Turning them guaranteed that the chicks didn't develop lopsided.

Jonathan was the egg turner. Nobody else had the patience.

As he carefully rotated each one so that the number showed or didn't show, he gave the class a running commentary on each future chick.

After a while the other guys adopted particular eggs, and the inevitable "my egg is better than yours" rivalries started up.

All this egg parenting made it hard when we "candled" the eggs to check on their progress. Everybody would huddle around in the dark as we placed an egg over a special light. The shell would glow night-light pink, and the embryo would be silhouetted.

If it was healthy, we might see a tiny beak, or an eye, or maybe a thin-clawed foot. Most times, it would shift with the heat of the light. Then cheers would go up, and the father of the egg would get his share of back-slapping.

But it wasn't always congratulations.

Over the twenty-eight days one egg had stopped developing. It didn't stir with the light's heat.

Cracking the egg open seemed like a good opportunity, one of those "teachable moments" supervisors practically salivate over, to give a quick lesson on the stages of gestation.

"Yo, man, you kilt it. Ya shoulda let it be. Maybe it was just sleeping."

"How could you murder such an innocent thing?"

"Take it easy, you guys," I rushed in to explain.

"Keep in mind, that there wasn't any movement when the egg was warmed, and that means it was dead."

The feathered lump was wet and bloody, and obviously had been dead for a while.

"God, that's disgusting."

"Man, I'm outta here. I'm gonna puke."

"What can I tell, they 'ain't havin' it' as the young *gentlemen* say these days," Officer Brink grunted after he finally got everybody calmed down with the threat of all-day lockdown.

Brink, a fastidious, disciplined, older Jamaican, was one of the COs who volunteered to work in the new program. He was always pressed and polished, his bald head as shiny as the combats he sported. He'd been a policeman in his beloved homeland for fifteen years before coming to the United States and had little patience with what he saw in America.

"They do things differently down there I tell you," he never tired of saying.

I'm sure they did, and I knew enough not to ask any questions.

I could easily imagine him in his pressed khaki uniform and black boots wielding a riding crop.

From the look on his lean tight face that morning I knew he had his own issues with the whole project. I understood Brink's uneasiness. He hated a mess.

But I was surprised by the kids' outrage and horror.

After all I knew each of their histories, their crimes, their blatant disregard for other people's lives. They sold crack to the sickest addict, or broke into old people's houses, tied them up, then stole their food money. Gun sales, knife fights, babies sired and abandoned, it didn't matter to them.

I mean, it was just a lifeless egg....

Then, looking at the bereaved faces staring at the floor, the wall, anywhere but at the wounded heap of a chick, I suddenly realized that cracking that shell had opened that deepest wound in each of them. They'd all, in one way or another, had childhoods as vulnerable as that dead chick's. They probably had been unwanted even before the pregnancy test came back positive. They'd been abandoned by their fathers, or mothers, and eventually sold into foster care, put into group homes, lost to the streets.

Jonathan saved the day.

"What about number fourteen?" he shouted out over the angry, unforgiving hush that filled the room.

"Yeah, what about mines?" DeAndrew, a nineteen-year-old stunted by years on heroin, asked in a squeaky voice. "I still bet ya it's gonna be twins."

And it was number fourteen that absorbed all of Jonathan's attention that first morning of hatching season.

But unlike the other guys, Jonathan hadn't played favorites. Over the twenty-eight days he never claimed an egg for himself. He just fathered them all.

I suspected he'd had enough of "favorites" while he was growing up.

He should've been one himself since he was the only man-child in a family of four sisters, youngest born at that. For some reason though, that even Jonathan couldn't explain, he was the family outcast.

His mother pretty much confirmed that view the first time I met her at our annual parents' night.

"The only reason she's coming," Jonathan told me, sounding angry and sullen as though she *wasn't* coming, "is because I'm in this dumb-ass program and she knows I'd get kicked out if she didn't.

"Not that I care one way or another," he quickly added.

Mrs. Franklin showed up in her LPN uniform.

"She just wanted to make sure everybody knew she was 'a professional' and really shouldn't have a kid in jail," Jonathan told me afterward.

He was right. That's exactly what she said after we shook hands and I tried to tell her about Jonathan's academic progress. She made it plain to me that for years she had worked all day and went to school at night until she finally got her nursing degree, and that each of her daughters was making her place in the world.

It was clear there wasn't any place in their world for a son and brother who sold drugs, slept on the streets, and finally got arrested this last time for robbing food off the loading dock of a Stop & Shop.

"There are a few things she left out," Jonathan snorted and told me the rest of the story.

"When I turned ten I got half a shelf in the refrigerator for my food."

Food he had to buy for himself with money he got from a paper route and the leftover change his sisters threw into a jelly jar for him.

"When school started in September, she'd take me to buy school clothes. Just that once. So that by June my legs and arms would be sticking out all over.

"I stopped going to school in junior high. I was sick of kids making fun of the way I looked. That's when I started hanging out on the streets, hustlin' to get money for clothes and stuff."

At first he'd steal the truant notices out of the mailbox. But after a while, when a few slipped through and his mother didn't say anything to him, he gave up and didn't worry about it.

And his mother and sisters did the same thing.

He was locked out of the house. They tossed the few things he had into a cardboard box and left it out on the fire escape.

"To rot as far as they were concerned," Jonathan said.

"That's when the family court thing started and I ended up in different group homes, and then Rikers and, well, you know all the rest," he finished off.

No wonder Jonathan was able to look so matter-of-factly at that matted-down lump of feathers that morning.

And no wonder he could be so devoted to all the hatchlings tentatively on their way.

There wasn't much time for thumb sucking after that first peep and final breakthrough of number fourteen. And not many chores got done as soon as word got out down the hall that delivery was at hand.

The expectant fathers came in and hovered over the incubator.

Eric, a sixteen-year-old who'd seen his own son born, kept nudging Miguel and mumbling, "There's always blood, man."

BeeBee, who'd been angriest about the cracked egg, stood right there making sure no more atrocities were committed.

They cheered as each chick bravely pecked through and stumbled into the world, wet, dazed, and hungry.

But Jonathan was clearly in charge.

As each newborn exhausted itself staggering around the incubator then falling down asleep, he carefully picked it up and put it in the cardboard box a few of the guys had lined with shredded paper and warmed with a heat light.

Paternity rights got thrown to the wind as soon as those chicks made their way into the big house. Everybody lost track of which chick came from which numbered egg. So a whole new series of adoptions took place.

Of course, chicks weren't the only things that hatched that morning.

There were arguments all over the place.

"I saw him first."

"Yo, man, what you doin', put my chick down."

"No way, bro, that one's mines, I swear that's number seven."

Mr. Brink quietly stood close by on the lookout for hands folding into fists.

Eventually each guy settled on a chick of his own, and the only fists I saw that day were the ones folded over the newborns.

No one argued with Jonathan about his chick because no one wanted it.

It had been number four, a brown egg that spent the morning rocking and being knocked about by all the other chicks. There was a pin-size hole in the shell and the dust-speck sight of a beak, but it was as though the newborn inside didn't have enough energy to hammer out.

Finally, Jonathan cracked the egg slightly with his fingernail. Then, after about a half hour with a little more help from him, the chick blundered into the world.

Unlike the others it couldn't stand up. One of its claws was turned in on itself so when it tried to stand or walk it fell on its face.

Jonathan reached into the incubator and scooped the chick up into his hand.

"I got mine," he announced proudly.

Everybody called it Cripple, but that didn't bother Jonathan. He happily spent hours massaging the tiny claw, helping it splay out.

The other dads took turns cleaning out the paper from the bottom of the "nursery."

"You think that's disgusting," Eric would chime in whenever one of the guys complained about the nursery mess, "wait till you got to change your kid's diaper and it's full of green shit."

During class time students settled into their own routines with their chicks. Tiny yellow heads peeked out of shirt pockets while others dozed in the crooks of their caretakers' arms as the guys tried to do math or write essays.

A great calm came over the big house during those nursery

days. Overnight a pen of young cocks had been transformed into a brood of mothering hens. Voices got softer, nobody cursed, threatened, got in your face. Suddenly the block was a place of protection and warmth.

That is until the day of the Big Race.

The hatchlings grew fast. Genes saw to that, along with a heat lamp, cornmeal mush, and a bowl of water the chicks walked through as often as they drank from.

Jonathan was the one who suggested the race in the courtyard.

"Good idea, Jon, and we'll have a Special Olympics for Cripple," DeAndrew joked, his hands still trembling even months after his heroin withdrawal.

"That's okay, Cold Turkey," Jonathan shot back. "Come Friday, we'll see. At least Cripple's brains aren't scrambled from all that shakin' you give yours."

The class roared and Jonathan triumphantly stuck his thumb in his mouth like Popeye with his corncob pipe.

Meanwhile, Eric suggested that the dads make paper airplanes.

"We can fly 'em after the chick race and see whose goes the best," he said.

Jonathan kept his paper creation as close to the chest as he did Cripple. He worked for hours on his plane with his back turned from the group. Unlike the other pilots who test-flew their planes across the room, Jonathan refused to show his craft before the race.

Then finally the day arrived.

Before we went out to the rec area we had to come up with a way of telling the chicks apart. They were too small for tags.

"How about each guy colors his chick's beak with a different marker," Turner, our resident graffiti artist, suggested.

"What about fumes?" Brink asked.

"Come on, sir, it ain't gonna hurt 'em. I been workin' with markers all my life, and look at me, I'm okay."

I quickly agreed. I could see the looks on the other guys' faces and knew where they'd go with that remark. I just hoped a little ink wouldn't do too much harm to the chicks.

Brink insisted the group march out single file into the courtyard.

"Sorry, Mr. C, I hate to be a wet blanket, but it's the only way I can keep these hoodlums under control," he explained.

They were an odd parody of the traditional chain gang, walking out one behind the other. But instead of a sledgehammer in one hand and pickax in the other, each young man carried a baby chick and a paper airplane.

Most of the other rec yards were shadeless, dusty courtyards.

But for some reason, the youthful offenders program was assigned to one of the nicer yards. Maybe it was Brink's influence. I could easily imagine him complaining to DOC in his clipped military voice that if they expected him to spend an hour a day outside doing PT with a bunch of young criminals, they needed to come up with some grass and a few shade trees.

However it came about, we got just that, along with a concrete picnic table, a full basketball court, and a dirt track encircling it all. It looked as though it should've had swings and slides and a double seesaw, and maybe even a wicker basket on the picnic table.

That flight of fancy, though, was cut short by the double roll of highly polished razor wire that ribboned around the courtyard like a sinister Slinky at the top of the tall chain-linked fence.

That day, though, we all had wings. I had my reveries, and my students had their airplanes and baby chicks, and Officer Brink had his sunshine.

Once the guys hit the outdoors they took off, running and shouting across the courtyard like little boys released for recess.

I looked nervously over at Brink. It seemed to me they were about to go up and over that wire cage.

But Brink just smiled at them as though there wasn't a "gangsta" among them.

"Don't worry," he offered some unaccustomed reassurance. "They'll wind down.

"Rodriguez, don't make a liar out of me," he interrupted himself. "Get off the picnic table."

And of course they did calm down.

They soon ran out of breath and collapsed on the grass under the tree. They were suddenly a Sunday school class ready to hear the Word.

"If it's okay, I think we should just let the chicks get used to being outside before we start the race," Jonathan announced.

The chicks were more disciplined than their dads. At first, they walked cautiously on the pincushion of stubbly grass or tried to climb up on their dads' pant legs and back into cradling hands. Eventually, after each guy gave his chick a first-day-of-school push, they wandered around pecking at invisible bugs.

But not Cripple. He leaned against Jonathan's stretched out leg.

With one thumb in his mouth and the other gently stroking Cripple's fragile head, Jonathan smiled slyly at the chicken chaos all around him.

"How am I supposed to know where it is?" Brink worked hard to snarl when Miguel ran up to him asking if he had seen his hatchling.

"Do I look like a lifeguard?"

Still Brink pointed over to the tree where three chicks were leapfrogging up the tree trunk.

Finally Brink had had enough chaos and gave a two-fingered whistle.

"Okay, you knuckleheads, listen up," he said.

"Get your chickens and stand over here."

I looked over at Jonathan. I was worried he was about to experience one more defeat in a life filled with them.

But not him. His smile cracked around his thumb and he gave me, of all things, a wet thumbs-up!

"I figure we'll have the race first, now that we've got the little guys under control, then we'll fly our planes," I explained to the brood.

"The best place, I think, is center court. What we'll do is on the count of three, you'll put your chick down then step back ten paces. All you can do is call to your chick. That's it. Nothing else.

You can't walk up to it, touch, nothing. The first chick to walk out of the circle is the winner."

"Mr. C, don't you think we should, like, test the court first? You know, make sure it's not too hot?" Eric suggested, the only one of the adoptive dads who had his own kid. "I mean, we wouldn't want the chicks fryin' their feet or anything."

"Good idea, Eric. Why don't you tell us if it's okay," I answered.

"Yeah, yeah, you gangstas, go ahead, laugh," Eric said, getting down on all fours and putting his wrist against the blacktop to test the temperature like it was a huge bottle of baby formula. "Wait till you got your own seed. You'll be doing all kinds of stuff you never done before."

"Just a little warm, Mr. C," he said, jumping to his feet. "I think we're ready to go."

"Jonathan, do you want to add anything?"

"No, except, maybe, may the best chick win."

At first the chick coaches were reluctant to lower their charges onto the sun-warmed blacktop, abandoning them to the fray. The guys stood facing each other and whispered into their cupped hands. Maybe they were remembering their own initiations to the streets, that first face-off.

"Okay, gentlemen, chicks close to the ground please," Mr. Brink called from outside the circle. "On your mark. One. Two. Three. Release."

Hands opened, chicks hit the court, the circle exploded, and the shouting began.

"Ten paces, ten paces," Mr. Brink kept yelling as the guys lurched and dodged and leaned forward, all the while calling out the color of their charges' beaks.

"Come on, Purple."

"Move, Green, move, over here, dumb ass."

"Yo, yo, Red, Red, it's me. Come to Papa."

At first the chicks moved as one feathered ball. They swarmed a little to the right, bumped to the left. A short stubby neck stretched up as lookout, scanned the edge of anxious faces, then disappeared into the clutch of its brothers.

Then, one by one, the chicks collapsed wherever they were.

"Shoot man, they're dead," BeeBee sputtered over the chorus of colors still being shouted out. "They're friggin' dead."

"Shut up, BeeBee. They can't be," DeAndrew shouted back.

"Yo, man, mine's on the move. Come on, Blue, come on, baby."

But even Blue gave up. Suddenly his legs folded, his eyelids shut, and his head lay on the hot macadam.

We all stared at the circle of feathers, stunned.

"They're not dead, you bunch of monkeys," Brink broke the silence. "They're just sleeping!"

Skeptical, the circle of disappointed coaches hunkered down, intense as crapshooters, and peered at their chicks.

"I think they're still breathing. Yeah, look yo, you can see them moving," Turner assured the others.

"You're right, Turner. They're just taking a nap in the sunshine," I said, allaying their fears. "The way you guys are always nodding off in class."

"But what about the race?" Eric whined. "It's dead, done, over."

"It ain't over yet, boys," Jonathan announced.

He had stood quietly on the sidelines during the race watching Cripple. The lame chick had sat center court, his withered claw tucked underneath his feathers while his bony head swiveled around.

Now Jonathan, still ten paces away, crouched down like a roosting bird himself, looked straight at Cripple, and softly clapped his cupped hands. Slowly Cripple stood up and started limping toward him.

We all watched in disbelief as Cripple staggered over the other chicks, ruffling sleeping feathers as he went. Once or twice he skidded against the hot pavement. But nothing seemed to stop him.

"Ju-das H. Priest. Will you look at that?" Brink whispered.

By then the runt of the litter had become everybody's adopted son and they all started shouting.

But not Jonathan.

He just squatted there, guiding his charge with his eyes and a smirk, until finally Cripple dropped into the warm cradle of his cupped hands and fell asleep.

"Special Olympics, hah, DeAndrew?" Jonathan said as he shot up from the ground, his hand and Cripple held high in the air.

"Yo, man, you got the best, no doubt," DeAndrew shouted above the cheers of the other guys as they swept up their own chicks and jumped around, whooping, taking turns pounding Jonathan on the back.

It was a while before Jonathan could break through his wide toothy grin and stick his thumb in his mouth. He sat on the picnic table in the shade and sipped at that thumb like it was a forty ounce of Olde English.

One by one the other chick dads settled down around him and grinned for the sheer pleasure of grinning.

But I suspect those smiles went deeper than that. Jail life festered with failure. Usually, inmates savored anyone's defeat—other prisoners or COs. Every once in a while, though, someone would get a letter from a long silent girlfriend, or a package of cookies, or a chance at a kitchen job, and the whole block would vibrate with good will.

"Well, men," I addressed the sleepy, smiling faces looking up at me.

"Looks like school's out for the day, and I think its nap time. What do you say?"

There were cheers and chicken cheeps to my suggestion. Naps were as precious as contraband cigarettes. But as the kids rolled up onto their feet, they seemed reluctant to leave.

Then a voice pleaded from behind me.

"But, Mr. C, what about the paper airplanes?"

It was Mr. Brink.

"I mean, you wouldn't want to waste the paper and all," he blustered, suddenly embarrassed by his enthusiasm.

"Yeah, come on, let's go," they all shouted.

And without a word from me they took charge. Lines were drawn, and fingers twitched, ready to let them fly. It wasn't a contest anymore. They had their two winners, Jonathan and his long-shot chick, Cripple. Instead they were satisfied to play like the boys they probably never were.

They stood poised on the edge of the grass, their construction paper planes held high between thumb and forefinger.

"All right, you thugs," Jonathan commanded. "On the count of five let 'em go."

"Five, four, three, two, one, blast off!"

A spring breeze showed mercy and lent a hand as planes dipped, soared, looped, and dove into the grass and concrete.

Jonathan's plane had been one of the first ones to smash up. It was shaped more like a boxcar than a jet. He only tried it once, then folded it up and put it in his back pocket. After that he shouted hints and gave suggestions, happily running to the far ends of the yard to lend a hand.

Nobody was surprised that DeAndrew's plane, launched with trembling fingers, got caught in the tangle of razor wire.

"Hey, what are you looking for, another charge?" Brink joked. "Attempted escape?"

"I can dream, can't I?" DeAndrew called back.

Slowly, those crumpled wings and pushed-in noses brought everything to a halt. Still no one abandoned their creations. Instead, they swooped down like rescue bombers and picked up their paper airplanes with the same tenderness they'd shown their chicks.

The boys trotted around the rec area one last time, across patches of brilliant sun and cool shade and shouted out to each other favorite lines from the latest rap song the way my friends and I would yell "olee-olee-in-free" and "ee-auk-ee" back and forth across the dark fields of long ago summer nights.

Jonathan was the last one to finish his lap of the courtyard. He jogged across the grass toward me, laughing and spinning his arms and legs like a pinwheel caught by the wind.

"Whoa, thanks, Mr. C!" he shouted out as he ran past me.

"That was the *best* party I've ever been to."

Then he sprinted off to catch up with the other guys as they disappeared one by one behind the huge metal door Brink had unlocked and held open.

"Come on, Mr. C," Brink shouted, impatiently clattering his jail keys.

"I have to get these characters back. They want their naps."

Slowly I made my way across the yard, reluctant to go into the jail and give up the sun and the breeze and what had happened out there.

"Party?" I thought as I moved toward Brink waving me in.

"The best one he'd ever been to?"

And then I remembered the boy Jonathan had described to me. The nappy hair, the scarecrow arms and legs sticking out of his too small pants and shirts, the ashy skin, the hungry mouth.

Who'd invite that kid to a party? He'd eat all your food! Smell up your house! Steal your silverware! Give the other kids head lice!

Yeah. Come to think of it, maybe Jonathan was right. Maybe that *was* the best party he had ever been to.

Chapter Fifteen

Meet the Author

No disrespect, Mr. C, but you're shittin' me, right? You really haven't read *Harry Potter and the Half-Blood Prince*, yet?" Dominic asked, back when we all were still worried about what would happen to Harry and all the rest of the good guys.

Dominic had "found" books in prison the way other inmates "find" God. But Dominic was a particular kind of zealot. He only read in jail, and he only read the Harry Potter books.

He wouldn't read anything else despite his obvious intelligence and my efforts to get him to branch out. He had discovered the series in jail, and that's where he read them, over and over again, until he could quote dialogue or discuss the finer points of plot. It didn't even matter to him anymore what order he read them in. It was whatever volume came his way.

"I haven't gotten around to it," I defended myself.

"You got to read it. I mean, I want to know what you think about... Well, I can't say until you've read it," he said, barely able to conceal his contempt for how backward I was.

At twenty, Dominic was good at contempt. He'd learned it in some of the best schools around. He'd been in any number of juvenile centers, local or county lockups, and state prisons since he was thirteen and his mother and father, the odd couple in the lives of the guys I taught—parents who were still together—gave up on him.

"I been locked up all along the East Coast, and not in any of those pussy places either," he'd brag to the young new jacks who gravitated to him. They were awed by the scars and tattoos he showed off, pulling up the sleeves and legs of his orange scrubs.

"And I tell you, man, you don't want to let the po-lice get your ass in North Carolina."

In his brief times out of jail between bids, Dominic had managed to father two boys, JoJo, four, and Antonio, eighteen months, miraculously, like some New Testament story, by the same young woman.

After his last stint upstate, Dominic had decided to move himself, JoJo, and Antonio with their mother down to Florida.

"Things were heatin' up and I knew the Yonkers' pigs were out to nail me on anything they could, so I cut out.

"I was working construction down in Florida, getting good money," Dominic would muse, "fucking good money."

Apparently, though, the money from pouring concrete wasn't quite good enough. He hit Interstate 95 one more time.

"I swore on my sons' lives that that was going to be it," Dominic said, sounding as wistful as somebody could with a rap sheet as long as his.

"My man Torro needed some stuff he'd bought off these Cuban dudes, real mean motherfuckers, transported up to Yonkers, so I said I'd do it.

"JoJo kept crying that he didn't want me to go. He said he wanted to come with me. I almost brought him. I figured it was only a shot up the road, might be fun for him, but I decided at the last minute not to. He was doing the potty thing pretty good, but I wasn't trustin' it."

Caught with guns and a kilo of coke in his trunk, Dominic was lucky that he was only looking at two years in the county pen. Plus an outstanding drug sales warrant in New Jersey. And once New York and New Jersey got finished with him, he had six months to do in the Florida system. Somehow, he dodged the feds. Even he was surprised.

"That's because the DA was so stupid," he sneered, looking a gift horse in the mouth.

Dominic didn't let it go until I finally gave in and read *Harry Potter and the Half-Blood Prince*.

Of course he wasn't satisfied. After I finished the book all he wanted to do was debate Dumbledore's fate and show me how wrong I was.

"Dumbledore's dead, gone," he'd hammer at my objections.

"Snape is one of the death-eaters, and he finally got Dumbledore out of the way."

It was strange having a conversation about magic and wizards and spells and death-eaters with a six foot five, muscled, Puerto Rican Italian with knife scars down his cheek and neck who sold drugs and guns to the highest bidder, no questions asked, and who had hurt people in ways I didn't want to know about.

It was a conversation you didn't expect to be having in the middle of a makeshift classroom with bars on the windows, doors locked, a cop in the room, red-buttoned emergency alarms on each wall, and two security phones programmed for immediate response if a receiver was left off the hook for thirty seconds.

But it was one Dominic insisted on having.

He never came up with any convincing evidence. It was just that his scenario fit the way he looked at the world. Life sucks. Evil always triumphs over good. Trust nobody, ever.

"Well, Dominic, you'll just have to wait until the last book comes out." I shrugged.

"Which means I'll have to get myself arrested again so I can read it," he said.

"You're not serious, are you?" I asked. "Just buy it or go to the library and read it. You love the books so much."

Dominic looked at me as though I was helping him plan his next gun run.

"Mr. Chura," he scoffed. "I don't read books in the world."

At least Dominic read, if only in jail. Most of the other guys were too busy playing cutthroat Monopoly, or watching Jerry Springer incite riots among his audience, or plotting fights against some scumbag who'd dissed them.

So the day I announced that a man who wrote a book about his life on the streets would be coming to class to talk to them, they were disinterested—and pretty skeptical.

"Why would some guy? Who wrote a book? Want to come here and talk to a bunch of hoodlums like us?" Dominic spit out.

"He must b-b-b-bee some k-k-kind of loser," Jimmy, who usually held his own counsel in class because of his stutter, managed to get out.

"He'd be too afraid to come to jail," Liam gave the favorite jailhouse boast. It was a funny remark coming from a hundred-pound carrottop who was terrified of everybody, COs and inmates alike.

"Afraid or not," I said, "he'll be here Friday morning."

They may've been disinterested and unconvinced, but they all scrutinized one of the two copies of the book I passed around.

One by one they stared into the author's grizzled, light-skinned, droopy, mustached face.

"Hey, Mr. C, this Leo guy's a crackhead from Yonkers." Kahlil looked up from reading the back of the book, his eyes suddenly sparked with interest. Kahlil had been in and out of jail a few times from when I first had him in class. This time back he was too old for school. But when he asked—begged, whined, Kahlil-style—of course I let him come as a visitor. "You can't let him come in here."

"No, Kahlil, if you look at what they're saying, Leo *had* been a crackhead. He isn't one anymore."

I hardly got the words out before they drowned me in a chorus of teeth suckings and "Yeah, sure"s.

"He probably copped from me when I was hustlin' down at the projects," Dominic snorted. "He's probably down there now scoring, droolin' all over himself."

Kahlil, who usually wasn't interested in anyone else's words but his own, was the only one who took the bait. He brought the book back to the block.

"This guy just got lucky," he said the next day, tossing the book down on the table.

"I mean, if that white guy hadn't picked up his stuff on the train and read it he'd still be living on the streets."

"Yeah, he was lucky," I countered, "but can he write?"

"Well, he is pretty good. I mean, there's a couple of places where he's talking about getting zooted that are, like, so real, I got high just reading 'em."

"Yo, give me that book. I'm taking it back and smokin' it." Dominic got a laugh.

As Leo tells his story, he was saved by a pencil stub and a bored editor.

He was a local boy just like these young men. He'd grown up in the suburbs of Manhattan, went to Yonkers high school, hung out on the local streets, was chased and harassed by the local police the way every other poor black kid in Yonkers was.

Somehow, though, he never ended up in county corrections like a lot of his friends. Instead, he slipped quietly and quickly beneath society's dragnet.

By the time he was twenty, his life was completely destroyed after a series of family crises, and crack had him crawling around the city's underbelly, living in its tunnels, subway stations, and derelict buildings.

One night, absolutely broke and fiending for some dope, he wrapped himself up in the dirty blankets he kept stashed on an abandoned subway platform. He took out a pencil stub he'd picked up earlier that day, thinking that maybe he could sell it, and for some reason started writing on some paper trash he used as a pillow exactly what it felt like when crack exploded in his brain.

But he didn't stop there.

He kept on writing, about the young whores he hung out with who were more haggard and desperate than he; about the other winos on the streets; and about Mother Francis, a roly-poly nun who came down to the Bowery every night in the winter in her brown robes and handed out sandwiches. Her hands were so twisted with rheumatism she could barely hold out the cup of coffee she offered him, but she always made him laugh.

Even after he got some coke the next morning (there was always some crackhead in worse shape than you; all you had to do was find one, beat the shit out of him, and take his stash) he kept writing.

Then Leo got the idea of showing his stuff to Collier, this guy who put out a four-page street newspaper and who got some of the down-and-outs like Leo to write for it. He didn't know what Collier's gig was; he obviously had money. Still, he published this paper every couple days, then hired street people to sell it. On a good day peddling papers, Leo could make enough for a McDonald's lunch.

Collier liked what he read and promised to print a few of his stories. Then he started asking Leo for more. After that Leo could buy a McDonald's and enough dope to keep him from getting really sick, like he usually was.

That's when this editor, a white guy from Connecticut, coming home from Manhattan after a long day, picked up a copy of the street newspaper somebody had left on the train and read one of Leo's pieces.

The next day he called Collier to find out who this Leo guy was.

Eventually Leo had a book contract and more money than he'd seen in years, more money than he knew what to do with.

Well, he knew what to do with it, but it wasn't good for him.

He got so wasted for weeks at a time that he missed two deadlines and almost blew the contract. Mother Francis jumped in, and Collier helped, so Leo did his first stint in rehab, then his second stint. Then the book came out.

Luck or talent, everybody was suddenly looking forward to Friday.

But they weren't surprised when Leo didn't show.

They'd been expecting that.

They took turns hectoring me.

"See, I told you."

"No author's gonna come to jail."

"He chickened out."

"He's probably still too stoned from last night."

Their harping sounded more relieved than disappointed. Leo not showing up sat better with them than some anonymous author coming voluntarily to the county lockup to talk to them.

Of course, they weren't interested in my explanations.

"The man had a late-night meeting at the group home where he's on the board of directors. That's something he does for *free* to help young kids like you guys. It takes a lot of time."

I was desperate to justify Leo's failure.

"So, he overslept and missed his bus. The next one would've gotten him here just before lunch, so I rescheduled for next Friday."

My excuses sounded pretty lame even to me, and I started to wonder if the guys' suspicions were right and worried about next Friday.

But a week later he was waiting at the gate right on time.

Leo looked exactly like his author picture.

His face was thin, drawn, and lined. His eyes were wide, as though wondering at the turn his life had taken, and watery, as though remembering everything he'd seen in darker times.

He was a tall man, but it took a while to realize it since he walked stooped over a middle-aged belly like someone accustomed to lugging around all his belongings in black plastic bags.

His pants were wrinkled and shiny, but surprisingly his shoes were new and buffed.

"Comes from years on the street." He laughed, following my gaze.

"Got to take care of the feet. Sometimes they're the only friends you got."

Most days my walk from the jail entrance to the classroom was a long one, down several hallways, through a half dozen gates, and up one floor on an old and overused elevator.

But that morning it was an even longer trek.

COs were slower noticing Leo and me at the gates; the ones who were always friendly were suddenly formal and distant. Our IDs were checked, and rechecked, and checked again, sometimes only a few feet down the hall. And at least two phone calls were made to the duty sergeant confirming Leo's visitor's pass.

At each delay, Leo was scrutinized, questioned, politely or not so politely, and in one or two cases harassed, all, of course, in the name of safety and security.

"You know, *sir*, this pass is only good until noon."

Officer Dorsten planted himself toe-to-toe in front of Leo, fingering the temporary ID pinned to his shirt pocket.

Officer Dorsten was always hostile to civilians. But to an outsider? Especially someone looking like Leo—a beat-up, worn down, black guy? He didn't stand a chance.

"Yes, sir, gotta be out by noon, I know," Leo answered, not missing a beat, his eyes on his shiny shoes.

"That's why I want to get to these young hoodlums as soon as I can, try to talk some sense into them knuckleheads, then get out of here."

"Well, that's twelve o'clock. Noon."

"Yes, sir, officer," Leo said, his stoop noticeably more pronounced.

Dorsten's bald white head pinked up.

He knew he'd been bested, but he didn't know how.

Reluctantly he stepped out of our way.

"You have a good day, officer," Leo rubbed it in.

I quickly hustled him toward the elevator, afraid that Dorsten would suddenly get the point of Leo's bowing and scraping.

"Sometimes, you gots to do what you gots to do," he whispered to me out of the side of his mouth as we got on the elevator.

But the suspicion that Leo met from corrections was nothing compared to what he encountered from my students.

When we got off the elevator I could see that the classroom was already packed, and I could hear through the thick safety-glass window that the place was humming like a hive. But as soon as I pushed open the door, the room fell silent and all heads turned in our direction.

"Okay youse guys, quiet down," Officer Ramos warned needlessly.

"This gentleman's got a lot of good stuff to tell you, so listen up."

Ramos had spent enough of his own time barely surviving on the streets of the Bronx to recognize a fellow traveler. He gave Leo a respectful, knowing nod, and in turn, Leo gave Ramos a firm, smiling handshake.

Dominic didn't miss that handshake or that smile.

He rolled his eyes at me, then grinned. "Gotcha!" that grin seemed to say. He had figured Leo out. He was 5-0, undercover for DOC. Now at least Dominic could sit back and enjoy the show.

But that was the last time anyone looked at me for the next hour.

Leo tugged at the legs of his already sagging pants, sat on the edge of the desk, and looked over a sea of doubting young faces.

"Good morning, gentlemen. I want you to know that I'm real happy to be here," he said and smiled.

No one smiled back.

Leo wasn't fazed. He'd broken through a lot tougher barriers than that wall of hostile, you-can't-tell-me-shit silence.

He took out a pair of drugstore half-moon reading glasses, flipped them open, and put them on the end of his nose.

He reached across the desk and picked up a copy of his book. He fanned the pages and smirked at his picture on the back.

"So, Mr. Chura's told you men that I wrote this here book, and you're thinking, big effin deal."

It was soon after that that Leo had them all up and out of that jail classroom and back on the streets.

He didn't preach. He didn't try to scare them. He didn't tell them they had to change. He just told them story after story.

He made it all so real they didn't even complain when he read whole pages from his book.

Listening to him, their palms sweated, their legs twitched, their bodies rocked. They leaned far forward, then suddenly lurched back as though they were the ones who took a bullet in the stomach instead of Leo's dope buddy, Lester, shot dead in the back by the cops while running away from an armed stickup.

"I warned Lester it was too risky when he told me about it," Leo said, shaking his head. "Lester'd be alive today if he didn't mess around with a heater.

"I got there just in time to hold my man as he died."

Leo left them kneeling on the pavement for a minute.

"That's why I always made it a point never to get involved with guns," Leo broke the spell. "Matter of fact, I never handled a gun in my life."

Of course they didn't believe him.

Suddenly backs were turned and hands raised in get-out-of-here waves.

Kahlil was the one to throw out the challenge. I was surprised since he was known jail-wide for being gullible and easy to goof on. Feeling bored? Just set Kahlil up with an outrageous story and the day flew by watching him run around like a cokehead desperate for blow, asking everybody, "Yo, man, did you hear that...?"

But that morning Kahlil put everybody's doubts into words.

"Sir. No disrespect. But you saying you never handled a gun, never-ever, in your whole life?" Kahlil asked, his hand slicing the air with each word like an umpire calling outs.

A string of "Yeah, right," "Bullshit," and "Keep it real," backed up Kahlil's protest.

Leo waited for the buzz to play itself out.

"You guys got to understand," he answered.

"I've done a lot of badass stuff in my life, half of it because I was stupid, the other half because crack made me do it, but something—I don't know what you'd call it—God, or Fate, or maybe hearing my mama inside my head warning me, 'Leo don't you dare or I'll whoop your black ass'—something kept me from ever picking up a gun.

"I know one thing, if I had, I wouldn't be here talking to you men. I wouldn't have written my book. I'd be dead or propped up in a wheelchair like a lot of guys I know."

The room fell silent as each of the guys ran through their own litany of friends and brothers and uncles shot dead, or as in Little Eddy's case, a father murdered by the mob right in front of him when he was six years old.

After that they couldn't hear enough about the coke and smack, about rolling white guys in the subway for cash, about the bitches, and about that long week of lovin' he had with some shorty in her apartment before the drugs finally robbed him of even his manhood.

But as much as they wanted to hear his battle-scarred stories, they kept circling back to that biggest, most mysterious story of them all, Leo's writing.

"Why'd you start writing that night you was so strung out? I woulda just got me a forty ounce and passed out."

"You get much loot for writing this book?"

"What it feel like, seeing your name in print. I mean I've seen my name in print plenty of times but that's just the po-lice blotter."

Leo fielded them all.

Before he answered a question, he'd ask the student his name. Usually inmates were reluctant to give their names, as though those simple syllables contained enough genetic information for the "gov'ment" to convict them of any crime it wanted.

But even though Leo made them nervous by asking, no one refused, no one countered, "Why you wanna know?" Instead, they suddenly became shy as little boys on Santa's lap and whispered their full names.

Then Leo would take off his glasses, maybe wipe his forehead with a dingy white handkerchief or take a sip of water, and consider his answer.

Some of these young men had been locked up on and off for years; so they weren't used to someone carefully picking their words when they spoke to them. And they certainly weren't used to having someone look right at them, not over their shoulder, not scanning the crowd for potential dangers, but at them.

"Whatever happened to that pencil stub?" Dominic couldn't help asking. By then Leo had him hooked good.

Leo laughed.

"Still got it. I don't get to write with it much anymore," he said.

"Got a computer. But you guys know how it is. You move up in the drug world, you don't dump the little man who helped you get where you are. Right?

"Anybody know what a talisman is?" Leo scanned the room for an answer.

Dominic nodded his head.

"Yeah, it's something that's got juice, you know, like magic," he answered.

"That's right. Well, that pencil stub was my talisman," Leo said.

Dominic had read enough Harry Potter to know how much power some simple, everyday object can have. Unlike the other guys he understood how a pencil stub, no bigger than a baby's finger, could be a portal into another world. It was the same way Harry and his friends—and enemies—could be transported from one place to another just by grabbing hold of a particular flowerpot or goblet.

But for the rest of those young boys, the only way they could make sense of that pencil stub was to think of it as though it were a joint. Just as chronic had rescued them from their own grimy dead-end lives of poverty and loss—at least for that lungful—that pencil was what had hauled Leo up out of the dark-tunneled subterranean world of crack into the light of something better.

"Okay, men, time to go back for chow," Ramos announced.

"Let's wrap things up. Mr. Leo's got to be out of here by noon, otherwise they'll be locking him up with youse guys."

There wasn't the usual mad rush for the door when Ramos called for chow.

Instead, the guys lined up to shake Leo's hand.

"Hey, Ramos, you got any extra paper around, I want the author's autograph," Kahlil said, setting off a major scramble for anything Leo could sign.

Then, just as deliberately as he had answered their questions, Leo wrote each student's name and a personal inscription on whatever they had scrounged up.

"Time, gentlemen, time," Ramos insisted. "Time."

One by one they left for the block. Some circled back for one last handshake. Some waved from the hallway through the security window.

"That's quite the crew you all have there," Leo said and shook his head. "Thanks, officer."

"No problem." Ramos nodded and looked at his watch.

"Sorry to rush you, Mr. C, but you better get going. You know what Dorsten's like. There's nothing the man likes better than causin' a stink, especially with civilians. Sorry, Mr. Leo."

"Gotcha, officer. I understand. Me and Officer Dorsten have already met." Leo chuckled and gave Ramos a firm handshake.

"You ready for this." I sighed.

"Piece of cake," Leo smirked, suddenly hunched as old Uncle Tom.

But before we got out the door, I saw Dominic through the security window coming down the hall from his block with something under his arm.

"What you doin' back here, papi?" Ramos scowled.

"Sorry, Ramos, but I was wondering if maybe . . ." he trailed off, his eyes darting sideways to Leo.

I'd never seen Dominic at a loss for words, but there he was, speechless.

"I was wondering, Mr. Leo," Dominic mumbled, then held out his copy of *Harry Potter and the Half-Blood Prince*, his own tattered, grimed-up talisman. "I was hoping you could sign this for me."

"Sure," Leo said. "I'd be happy to."

Without looking at anyone but Dominic, he opened the book to the torn title page.

"Dominic, right?" Leo asked.

"Yes, sir." Dominic nodded.

Leo clicked his pen and wrote several lines.

"Here you go, son," he said, handing the novel back to him.

The way Dominic held on to the book, gripping it with both hands, I expected him to be swirled away—back to Florida, to Disney World with his two young sons, maybe even to Hogwarts itself—to anywhere but the county jail.

Then, without looking up, he carefully opened the book, read Leo's inscription, and smiled.

Suddenly Dominic looked like a boy who had finally met a real wizard.

Chapter Sixteen

Visiting Room

Officer Peoples worked the visitors' lobby like a barker at a carnival sideshow.

"Number four hundred and seventy-nine, please. Number four hundred and seventy-nine, next, please," his baritone boomed out.

"Ma'am, are you number four hundred and seventy-nine? No? Then wait your turn," he said, his bellow turning into a bark.

A short woman dressed like a ball of black yarn stared up at him over the high counter, waving a legal-size paper in his face, pleading in Spanish.

There was more fear and confusion in her voice than pushiness. But Officer Peoples didn't seem to catch the difference.

"If you're not number four hundred and seventy-nine, I can't help you."

His bark was suddenly more clipped—like a man tired of doing his job.

Finally a younger woman no more than sixteen, her hair as black as the older woman's widow's weeds came up to her. Shifting a toddler from hip to hip the way some young girls casually toss a Gucci bag from shoulder to shoulder, she leaned over and whispered something to the woman, then led her away to one of those beat-up vinyl benches.

"Last call for number four-seven-nine."

Peoples shook his head in evident disgust.

"Okay, number four hundred and ninety, please. Number four hundred and ninety, next, please."

He was a short man, or so it seemed, the way he loomed over the counter, as though he were standing on a platform looking down at the crowd of mostly women visitors gathered below him.

He was meticulously dressed. Although it was hard to tell where his barrel chest ended and his pot belly began, his blue uniform shirt was carefully pressed and fit him perfectly, and his almond brown skin was smooth and shiny. His nameplate was polished; his silver badge looked newly minted. Although it was a style that had long played itself out on '80s TV, his black hair was jerry curled. He was obviously proud of it, since every once in a while he'd pat the swirl of glistening curls.

There was no doubt about it. The man knew how to dress.

But most of the visitors didn't.

At least by DOC standards.

Even though there were signs posted in English and Spanish all over the lobby with a dress code: No low-cut blouses. No skirts above the knee or slits anywhere, front, back, side. No shorts of any kind. No skintight anything. The less skin showing the better—the women, no matter what size, shape, race, or age, looked as though they had had their clothes painted on them. Their jeans and halter tops and blouses were so formfitting it was hard to imagine even a postage stamp being smuggled in in cleavage or waistbands that tight.

"You'll have to button that shirt up, miss. All the way to the neck." Officer Peoples sounded as though he was talking in his sleep.

"I don't care if you *are* his sister. You could be his great-grand-mother, for all I care. You are not going in there like that. Button up."

If he couldn't see a way to remedy the outfit, he turned the woman away, as cut and dry as his call for the next number. He ignored the curses spit at him in Spanish or in English, and he didn't bother to ward off the evil eye that stabbed his way.

"Number five hundred and eleven, please. Number five hundred and eleven, next, please."

Jewelry wasn't an issue until the women went through the metal detector. That's when he insisted—or rather the sensor did, it was so delicately set—that it all come off.

"Please remove all watches, crosses, rings, earrings, lip rings, nose rings, toe rings, belly-button rings, bracelets, chains, ankle bracelets," he intoned with each new visitor.

It seemed an odd litany to hear droned by a man who himself was decked out in a gold-link bracelet; a garnet pinkie ring; a wide, ornate, gold wedding band; and a Rolex that was more a piece of hardware than a watch. Even his tie clip was gold instead of the standard-issue tarnished silver bar.

"Look, young lady, your tongue hole won't close up in an hour," he'd snarl.

"And if it does, that's the way it goes. If you want to get in to see your boyfriend, then it comes out. No. Metal. Anywhere. Period."

None of the signs said anything about jewelry not being allowed in the visiting room. Still the women didn't dare point that out to him. They didn't challenge him on this, the same way they didn't question him on any of his other decisions.

They didn't seem resourceful enough or brave enough or feisty enough to do that. They were too desperate to get in to see their man or their son or their grandson or their nephew.

Or maybe they were just too beaten down from all those years of sitting and waiting in lobbies just like this one; or the long ride to get there, transferring from subway to train to bus after bus after bus; or the months of taking care of his baby on their own; or having to work two jobs to feed his kids and pay the rent because he wasn't out there bringing in any money, legal or illegal, they didn't care.

They knew they had to get past this Peoples guy first; that he was the one who would let them in or send them right back out onto the 42 bus to then transfer back onto the midtown 15 bus.

There was no sense in arguing. The clock had already hacked away enough of their allotted two hours in the visiting room.

So they'd tug their tank tops up, tuck their blouses in, strip off every piece of metal they had on. They'd kick off shoes, and shake out hair carefully tacked in place with hairpins. Some of them even had to slip out of their push-up bras.

They did whatever this man told them they had to do.

Of course, coats, sweaters, shoulder bags, shopping bags, or backpacks weren't allowed, anything in which contraband could be smuggled in or out.

Corrections had lockers the visitors could use, for a price. If they'd been there enough times, the women learned that the best ones were next to the officer's desk or, even better, a little behind it. Those were the ones that were certain to work. The others, the ones more out in the lobby, were all banged up and dented out of kilter from years of use, or of frustration, or of pent-up anger so that their blue metal doors stuck and their locks jammed.

The women and girls stuffed their purses and wallets and back-packs, their rings and chains and belts into the cubicles. Then they hip slammed them, shoved them, pounded them, knocked the door shut, and hoped they could get them open again because that's where their bus passes were and their money and picture IDs and apartment keys.

Once they'd gotten rid of their bags and jackets, they didn't know what to do with the locker keys. They ended up slipping them into the pockets of their snug jeans. They'd feel for them nervously over and over again to make sure they were really there as they stood waiting at one more sliding glass and metal door for yet an-other CO, this one sealed inside a windowed booth, to buzz the door open and finally let them into the visiting room.

That was the jail ritual, twice a day, two hours in the afternoon and two hours at night, four days a week, year after year after year.

But that wasn't the way it was outside on the walkway leading up to the jail.

There, those same mothers and grandmothers, aunties and friends, who knew each other from the neighborhood, or the proj-ects, or church, or years in and out of other visiting rooms, would often link arms and talk and laugh as they strolled along that tree-lined path coming up from the bus stop.

It didn't matter what language the women gabbled in—English or Spanish or Italian or Armenian or Jamaican or Haitian—they all figured out what those DOC signs posted along the way warned: keep it moving, don't respond to any inmate calling out, don't wave or gesture in any way, all on penalty of arrest.

Of course, they heard those shouts and calls coming from the five floors of cells looming in front of them.

There wasn't any way they couldn't.

But they still ignored them, as painful as it was.

What if it was their Miguel calling for his mamita? Or their Timmy trying to get grandma's attention? Or their Jamal or Arthur or Trayvel locked up, locked so far away from them? It was better not to think about that.

Instead they just kept chatting and arguing and joking. All that was missing was the kitchen table to talk over and the pots of black coffee or overly sweet tea to sip.

They didn't fall silent and drift apart until the jail's long shadow fell at their feet and Officer Peoples's voice bellowed out numbers all the way to the front door.

But the younger women, girls really, coming up behind them, making that same long walk twice a week, understood exactly what the signs said.

The difference was they just didn't give a shit. They'd do whatever they wanted and stop wherever the fuck they wanted.

They could have been anywhere—the mall, the Laundromat, the corner bodega, the edge of the park, or the basketball court, sitting, standing, strutting, waiting for the boys to show up, to notice them.

They walked up that sidewalk, two, three, four abreast, laughing and gossiping and yelling over one another.

Nobody listened to anybody. They shouted into their cell phones, and blasted their iPods so that the bass, the beat, the pounding voice of hip-hop vibrated the gold hoop earrings they wore two or three to an ear, some as big as a forearm.

They'd stop in the middle of the path to brush their hair or to fix a wedgie.

They even leaned against the very signs telling them not to congregate while one of the girls rummaged through her big leather bag looking for a cigarette.

"Girlfriend, you better not have any shit in that bag 'cept some Newports and a couple tampons," one of them would squeal.

Then they'd all look nervously over their shoulders and titter.

By then girlfriend would be cursing up a storm because she couldn't find a cigarette no matter how deep she dug, or the other girls would be cursing her because she didn't have any to spare.

But just like the mamitas and grandmas and aunties, they didn't answer the guys whistling and hollering down to them although that didn't stop them from parsing every single syllable of the cat-calls and the come-ons.

"Yo, bitch! Give me some of that!"

"Hey, mama, shake that fat ass!"

"Sit on this, shorty; you know you open!"

And when some guy called out one of their names, "Yo, Tabitha or Mylenka or Freda, I got something you want," they'd shriek and giggle like ten-year-olds even though they knew there'd be shit to pay if boyfriend heard about it, which was pretty stupid and unfair, since he had to be the one who was talking about her, spreading her name around the jail, the way he accused her of spreading *it* around the hood.

They heard every word those guys shouted but they didn't yell anything back. Every girl who ever went up that walkway knew by heart what happened to that stupid bitch, Yvette, when she did.

They'd tell each other the story over and over again, how that ho from Yonkers—the one with the three babies? All by different guys?—got arrested for hollering back to some crackhead who kept screaming that he wanted to fuck her.

She told him to come and get it if he wanted it so bad.

That's all. No big shit. At least that was how that slut, Yvette, said it went down.

That wasn't the way the DOC po-lice saw it.

They came screeching up in a squad car and threw her into the backseat and booked her, just for yelling.

Well...and maybe peeling her jeans down and mooning the guy. Nobody saw her do that, though, so that's just what the po-lice said.

These girls might've been dumb, but they weren't stupid.

They didn't shout anything back, but they still sashayed a little more slowly along the walk, and gave their tight-jeaned butts a little more wobble and their oversize titties a little more jiggle.

Once they got inside, though, they became those ten-year-old girls again, not the giggling kind, but the scared kind who did whatever The Man told them to do.

Things were different with the girls pushing strollers up that walk, or lugging baby carriers, or pulling toddlers along by the arm.

They still traveled in twos and threes. They still talked on their cell phones. They were still as loud as the gaggles of females up ahead of them.

But those young mothers, frustrated, exasperated, fed up with crying babies or whiny toddlers, didn't have much to say except to yell at their kids, or shout into their phones at those nagging so-cial workers who were always in your business, or curse out those bitches hot on their boyfriends who had the nerve to call them, threatening to tell him how they'd been hoing around while he was locked up.

If they did talk to each other it was to complain about how tired they always felt, or how they never got their SSI checks on time, or how their mothers wouldn't take care of the baby, not even for a couple of fuckin' hours, so they could go clubbing.

Walking up to the jail, they could've made fun of LuSandra's big butt, which had gotten even bigger ever since she had the twins, or Eldora's blown-up boobs, which were always sore from one more male mouth hungry to feed off her.

But they didn't, because they all knew what goes 'round, comes 'round.

"I don't know how you're goin' explain *that* to Dipper's daddy," one of them might say, pointing to the melon-size stomach that steered Daisy up the walk. If one of them did say something like that they wouldn't be joking. They were all worried about Daisy. There she was dragging two-year-old Dipper behind her, and now she was pregnant again, and Dipper's daddy locked up way too long to have planted that seed growing inside her.

If they did laugh it was more a rueful laugh. There wasn't anything funny about their lives.

The little kids were the ones who had the fun, kids like Tito.

Twice a week his mother would get him ready to make that long trip to see his seventeen-year-old daddy. She polished him up like a valuable stone so that his walnut complexion would shine, and dressed him in his stiff new jeans and Yankees jacket.

Tito was still shaky on his three-year-old feet despite his new Jordans, the ones with *real* laces not the usual Velcro straps for toddlers, because Tito's daddy insisted, "No son of mines is goin' walk around with baby sneakers."

Of course all Tito wanted to do on that jail path was stop and pick up cigarette butts and put them in his mouth. It didn't matter how many times his mother yanked him up by the collar, slapped his hand, or struggled to pry open his fist tight with three-year-old rage and determination. Before she knew it he'd be down in the dirt again.

Or there was two-year-old Sasha Marie who didn't *want* to sit in the stroller. "Me push, me push."

Her daddy never saw her in the same dress. They were always pink, baby blue, or yellow, his favorite colors, and stiff and frilly the way he liked them.

She loved being passed around by her mother's teenage girl-friends who painted and dressed her up like a doll.

Sasha Marie was a regular little lady.

That is, when she wasn't fighting her mother's grabbing, yanking hand. Once she was out of her mother's reach, she'd turn, shake her brown frizzled-hair pigtails from side to side, then giggle as she ran ahead.

"You're just like your fucking father," her mother screamed after her, "always doin' what you damn well please."

Even the infants in elaborate car seats were having a better time than their mothers who hauled those carriers around like grocery baskets.

The babies would smile and chortle over the latest trick their toes had performed, drooling spit-up oatmeal on their "Daddy's Little Girl" bibs.

After seeing this parade of strollers and toddlers, it was easy to forget that this was a jail and not a daycare center, and that going to see Daddy in prison wasn't a field trip like a visit to the post office or the supermarket recommended by the Head Start curriculum.

But Officer Peoples quickly dispelled that delusion.

Toddlers and babies were searched. Diaper bags and car seats were just more packages to be examined and cleared, or checked into a locker.

And he wasn't impressed with the likes of a Tito or a Sasha Marie.

He didn't think they were cute.

Matter-of-fact, he didn't think they should be allowed in at all.

You wouldn't believe the shit, and not the diaper kind, that these women tried to sneak in using their kids as couriers.

Besides, given enough years of coming in and out of a place like this, he figured he'd see those same kids eventually locked up just like their daddies and their uncles and their cousins and their granddaddies.

Really, though, what the hell did he care?

It was job security, guaranteed to get him to retirement.

"Number six hundred and forty, please. Number six hundred and forty, next, please," Officer Peoples called out over the whimpering babies, the whispering old ladies, and the girls cursing under their breath because they were dying for a smoke.

"Last call for number six-four-zero.

"Okay by me, ladies. You're wasting your own precious time." He'd give an exasperated sigh.

"Number six hundred and fifty-six, please. Number six hundred and fifty-six, next, please."

Chapter Seventeen
Grand Opening

There was everything but the ribbon to cut.

The county exec was saving that for the media. After all, he was the one who'd convinced the voters to approve the multimillion-dollar bond he needed to build the SHU, the county jail's newly designed special housing unit, a maximum security isolation block for the worst inmates.

Except for the ribbon, it had all the markings of a grand opening celebration. There were fancy pastries, bottled water, and freshly brewed coffee and tea.

It certainly wasn't what any of us expected. We knew our place. We were just a bunch of civilians—medical staff, teachers, and clergy—who were being given a sneak preview of the unit.

But that didn't stop any of us from filling our plates and cups. Maybe everyone else was like me and remembered the stale dough-nuts and tar-thick coffee I had had at my initial orientation to jail-house life almost a decade ago.

Once we'd sampled what we wanted, Warden Root, the warden in charge of the new construction, asked us to take a seat around a large mahogany conference table.

It was a fairly democratic gathering for DOC. There were no uniforms evident, no distinguishing dark blue shirts for sergeants or white shirts for captains. Instead it was opened collar oxford button-downs and pressed slacks. The only signs of rank were the gold shields all officers were required to wear on their belt loops and, of course, the warden's necktie.

Warden Root was young to be a top administrator in county

corrections. But he'd started working there in maintenance when he was nineteen and gradually made his way up through the ranks of the jail bureaucracy.

"How to hell do you think I got where I am?" he'd quip.

"I wasn't just learning different jobs over those years. I was busy picking up all the dirt on everybody along the way."

Warden Root didn't take anything too seriously. Including himself.

But we found out that day he was real serious about the SHU.

He introduced his crew of officers, architects, and engineers.

I'd never heard so many first names in all my years at the county lockup, an institution where surnames were the only ones anyone seemed comfortable with.

Each introduction became a riff on the months of construction they had endured together, the nicknames they'd invented for each other, the blunders made, the disasters avoided, or perhaps, not avoided, no one was saying.

The warden's crew laughed even before he finished his sentences. They were like people who've seen the same movie over and over again and can recite the dialogue to each other.

We civilians joined in, despite not knowing what was really so funny. We just enjoyed the friendly repartee and the feeling of being included by people who routinely excluded us.

Of course being a grand opening of sorts, there were speeches, charts, and color-coded graphs. We were each given a folder with a detailed description of the special housing unit's role in DOC.

The SHU, we read, was a state-of-the art highest security detention facility where the most dangerous and disruptive inmates were contained and isolated. Everything was designed to ensure the safety and security of the inmate and the staff working with him.

"People will be coming from all over the country to see what we've done here," Warden Root told us, suddenly solemn with the import of what he and these men had accomplished.

Then we got our hard hats.

"Since it is still officially considered a construction site, we're all required to wear these little mothers," Warden Root called out over the hubbub of everyone grabbing a hat, swallowing a last gulp of coffee, putting on coats, and getting backpacks, purses, and plastic bags.

There were lots of jokes about how silly we all looked—and felt—in the "one-size-fits-all" (which clearly wasn't the case) helmets. The nurses complained that the yellow clashed with their colored smocks, while we teachers said we should wear them in the classroom. Father Gabe, one of the prison chaplains, confessed that he kind of liked his. "It makes me feel like Father Mulcahy in *M*A*S*H*."

We walked down the penitentiary hallway huddled behind Warden Root, louder and sillier than we would ever think of being during our regular workday.

But once we made it past the SHU's first security gate, waiting in the sally port for the other door to open, we fell silent. The jokes and comments stopped. People moved away from each other and stood alone. The light was muted, the walls were freshly painted a pastel blue, and the air was cool and clean.

Slowly we could feel the noise, tension, and chaos of the rest of the jail slipping away.

When the second glass and metal door slid open, we stepped into the hallway next to the high-tech control desk and stood staring down two long corridors at right angles to each other, each side lined with cells.

There was something solemn about the place.

There were none of the clankings and gratings of the rest of the jail's metal-barred gates. There was no PA system jangling everybody's nerves with nonsensical announcements or static feedback. And you could hear, if you held your breath, which the place made you want to do so as not to disturb things, the faint *swish, swish, swish* of an ultramodern air system.

The cement block walls were a smoky gray; the floors tiled and glossy with wax; the lights, recessed and fluorescent.

Even though the block was unoccupied, no one spoke above a whisper.

"Each cell is monitored visually here on this panel," Warden Root said, pointing to the control desk lined with glowing mini-screens. "Plus an inmate can communicate with the officer through an intercom in his cell.

"The hallways are also equipped with cameras and wired for sound." He pointed to various corners and ceiling openings.

"So watch what you say," he said with an impish look in his eyes.

The cells were positioned so that they weren't directly across from one another. That way, inmates couldn't see each other, although they were completely visible to anyone in the corridor. The glass that fronted each cubicle was as thick as the steel beams that framed it. The walls were painted cream, while the entire steel framework was maroon. Each door had a slot where food trays were slipped through. But even that had a metal flap that hinged down and could be locked on the outside, so the cell, and the inmate, was tightly sealed off.

"Any of you who've worked in the old jail, especially with the minors, know the different kinds of mischief inmates can get into," Warden Root said, unlocking the door of one of the cells.

"You know the type of thing I'm talking about. The stuffed-up toilets, the faucets going full blast so the block gets flooded. Hitting each other with telephone receivers. Taking the showerheads apart and using the metal pieces for weapons. That kind of thing," he said, reciting a litany we'd all heard before.

"Not to mention what they do with their feces." He screwed up his face like a parent changing a messy diaper.

"We've addressed all those safety and security issues here."

He swept his arm across the cubicle like a real estate agent.

"An inmate never needs to leave his cell except for visits and court, and even then his arms and legs are shackled, and he's escorted by two officers. He eats, showers, sleeps, and does the other *s* word right here.

"The showerhead is set into the wall so there's nothing to take apart," he pointed out, running his hand along the smooth surface of the stall.

"His shower is turned on and off by the officer at the control desk, and his toilet is flushed the same way.

"Each cell is equipped with a phone. That way an inmate doesn't have to leave the holding area to make legal or personal calls."

Here Warden Root paused and watched us scan the cell for signs of a telephone.

He smiled, pleased with himself.

Then he moved over to the wall at the foot of the bed and pointed to two small grates flush against the concrete.

"One's an earpiece, the other's the mouthpiece. Simple, eh?

"Numbers are dialed by the officer and calls are terminated by the officer."

He shrugged. "Sometimes you got to do that, help a guy out of a tight situation by hanging up the phone for him when he's getting all crazy with his girlfriend, or his moms, or his lawyer."

"What's the button next to the speaker part for?" a nurse asked, pointing to a metal tab in the wall.

"Ah, good question." The warden beamed. "That's for the intercom, to call the officer at the desk."

He moved over to the cell wall to another sliding metal door.

"Now, as you all know, state regs mandate that a detainee must have at least one hour of rec per day," he said. "The way things are in the regular jail blocks with staffing issues, space problems, and weather restrictions, that's pretty much all they get.

"But the SHU inmates are lucky. They can have as much rec as they want, regardless of the weather or the usual rec schedule."

Next to each cell was an empty enclosure connected by a sliding metal door.

Warden Root pressed the intercom button and the door clanked open.

The rec area wasn't really any bigger than the inmate's living space; it just seemed that way without the sleeping pallet, the sink, the toilet, and the shower cubicle. Unlike the cell, however, its outside wall was thick, frosted glass with steel framing. It was opened at the top with a metal grate covering it. There was no equipment, no mats for working out, just the concrete floor.

"All an inmate has to do is buzz the officer on duty like I did and ask him to pop the door and out he goes. He can have rec all day long if that's what he wants."

Several of us walked around this echoing cube over to the grated windows.

You'd have to be pretty tall to see over the top of the glass barrier. Even if you could, the metal mesh was tight enough that you wouldn't be able to make out much of anything. Not that there was much to see, just some high-tension power lines, and a dusty field deeply rutted from dump trucks and construction vehicles.

There was, though, sunlight and fresh air and a strange sense of freedom after the constraint of the cell.

"Any questions?" The warden scanned the group.

No one said anything.

Instead we all moved quickly out of the cell and toward the doors, ready to head home.

Warden Root stood at the entrance, shaking each of our hands as we left the unit.

"Come back and see us real soon," he joked.

After the tour I had a hard time thinking of the SHU as a punishment.

I'd spent enough time on the regular blocks to know that the noise and smell were assaultive and relentless. As soon as you walked through the door, it hit you, and there wasn't any place to go to get away from it.

Two televisions booming, one in English, the other in Spanish.

People yelling down from the tier, or yelling across to each other at a table. Someone hollering into a phone, shouting for everybody to shut the fuck up because he couldn't hear. The security phone ringing. The CO bellowing out names for sick call, visits, haircuts. Showers hissing and toilets gurgling.

And no matter how hard the men tried, the blocks stank. Forty male bodies sleeping in bunks three feet apart can't help but smell of sweat, shit, piss, sex, and bad breath. And all the meals, no matter what was served, smelled of rancid meat and overripe fruit.

Somehow the quiet, the peace of having a cell to yourself; the air scrubbed clean by filters; the floors polished; the walls freshly painted; everything new and pristine in a place otherwise haunted by the lives of thousands of inmates stretching back to 1914; the sunlight filling up your space; just the words, "your space," where usually nothing is "yours," where "space" only exists inside your head, if you're lucky—all these things, it seemed to me, made the SHU appealing, somewhere you'd prefer to be, somewhere that the emergency response team wouldn't have to drag you into.

The first few times I visited students there, when the SHU first had opened up and was still a commodity of pride and an object of curiosity, even among the inmates, things were much the same as at our grand opening tour: clean, calm, and serene.

Even Officer Saner, the CO assigned to the new post, was on his best behavior.

Usually Saner held everyone in contempt. It didn't matter who you were or what your rank—inmates, civilians, other COs, sergeants, captains, the occasional warden—we were all the same to him. His disdain permanently curled his lips into a sneer; and his shaved head made him look even more imperious than he was.

But even he was under the spell of all that new furniture, the high-tech equipment, and the fancy gadgets. He'd stand up when you came into the unit, greet you, and ask how he could help.

And the young kids I visited there went through their own transformation.

They kept their cells neat. They made their beds, sheets tight and crisp. They stacked their books and magazines neatly on the high windowsills and stored their rolled up towels next to the books.

Unlike on the regular blocks, they were allowed to wear sweatpants and sweatshirts stamped with the county initials because, as Officer Saner politely explained to me when I mentioned how cold the unit felt, "I know, sir. They're still working on climate control."

My students appreciated the visits and the materials I brought them.

They'd ask how I was, how class was going, how Ramos and O'Shay were doing.

They'd thank me for coming, and hoped I'd visit again soon. And I did, as often as I could.

At the end of my own chaotic and frantic day in the classroom, I'd scoop up whatever magazines I had around—*National Geographic, Junior Scholastic, Science Today*—and head out to the SHU.

Once past the first security door, I felt myself decompress as I waited in the sally port.

The guys were happy to see me. They didn't curse or shout or rap incessantly the way they did when they were in class. Instead, they were soft-spoken.

And they did something they rarely did in the classroom. They listened to me. They attended to what I said. When I talked, they looked at me intently, as though they were reading my lips.

Then when it was time for me to go, they'd watch me walk down the hallway, pressing their faces at odd angles against the glass so they could follow me out.

It was only after I had been visiting the SHU for a while that I began to see things differently.

At first I thought the change in my students' behavior was the results of the SHU's calmer, cleaner, and more orderly environment.

But more and more I realized it was, in fact, the result of their total isolation.

They listened to me, they studied my face, they begged me to come back, they watched me leave, because they were hungry, hungry for words, hungry for sounds, hungry for the sight of people, any stimulation that broke their solitude.

And over the months that followed, the place itself began to show this underbelly of deprivation.

Conditions deteriorated. The walls got scuffed and nicked where inmates struggled against the ERT carrying them in. The floors still shone, but the windows didn't. They were smeared with hands and faces pressed against the glass.

Gradually, inmates stopped making their beds. They piled clothes on the floor. They left books and papers wherever they dropped.

Now when I visited after class some of my students would be sleeping. They'd bury themselves under the covers, their heads wrapped up in towels for warmth and to shut out the light.

If I was able to get them awake at all, calling through the tray slot, they'd grumble and splutter to be left alone.

Once they knew it was me and got up, they were still polite and appreciative of my being there, but they would stare, stunned and bewildered, wondering if I was real or just part of some dream.

And they were dirty.

Even the guys who were usually fastidious about how they looked became sloppy and disheveled. Like Pinto. When I had him in class, he'd arrive every day washed, shaved, and lathered up with Old Spice deodorant. His county oranges would be pressed, and his hair clipped short and brushed to a black lacquer.

But in the SHU, his eyes became puffy and crusted from endless hours of sleep. His face was covered with a patchy, scruffy beard, and his hair was knotted and woolly. When he leaned down to talk to me his breath was sour, and the odor of his unwashed clothes and body rose out of the metal opening like a malevolent genie.

That same foul, stale smell of soiled sheets, and unwashed armpits and assholes, began to pervade the whole unit. It hit you as soon as you walked into the SHU despite its turbogenerated air system.

But that wasn't the only thing that hit you when you left the sally port.

There was the noise.

Although many of the men had turned day into night, those who weren't sleeping would be screaming.

In typical jailhouse ingenuity, SHU inmates had figured out that they could still talk to each other, if they went out to their rec decks and plastered themselves right against the wire mesh and shrieked at the top of their lungs.

It might've been hard to distinguish the words, to really make sense of what the other guy was saying, but that didn't matter. One human was still communicating with another, connecting to someone just like him, someone living with the same sense of loss and isolation as he was. And all that screeching had an added advantage: DOC couldn't do a damn thing to stop it.

Officer Saner wasn't far behind in this steady deterioration, although in his case it wasn't so much a decline as reversion to his usual ways.

After a while he realized that once the ERT put an inmate in the cell, that's where he stayed. Saner was the one who decided whether he'd satisfy a man's request or not. All he had to do was push buttons, or, of course, he could just ignore the whole bunch of them.

His helpful attitude toward me vanished.

Suddenly he refused to give out certain materials that up until then he'd been allowing through, saying that they were contraband; or he insisted that the school provide certain supplies that DOC furnished before.

He got to the point where he barely acknowledged my presence.

Fortified behind the bank of controls and monitors, he didn't bother to look up from the motorcycle magazine he was reading. Instead, he'd let me stand there a minute or two.

Then he'd point to the top of the desk panel for me to leave the work and flick his fingers dismissing me. Or he'd tell me to come back at a "better time" when he wasn't so busy.

With each refusal he invoked safety and security issues.

"All I can recommend is that you talk to my superiors if there's a problem. Sir," he'd snicker, knowing that none of us civilians were stupid enough to do something like that if we ever wanted to get any business done in the SHU.

Eventually, inevitably, the grand, open feel of the SHU became as closed and claustrophobic as the rest of the jail.

The tours stopped, the inquiring visitors became fewer.

The muddy, torn-up, and rutted field around the SHU, just visible beyond the wire mesh of the rec cells, filled in with weeds and tattered plastic bags.

There wasn't any more talk about getting in truckloads of top soil and seeding it with grass, maybe planting a few flowering trees. Warden Root was too busy. He was knee-deep in blueprints and price estimates, iron girders and concrete frames, managing the county's next construction project, a model unit dedicated to inmate job training.

Slowly the SHU filled up with inmates—men, boys, old-timers, and fresh new jacks—scared and pissed as hell.

They slept their days into night.

They tried to shout and scream their loneliness away.

They abandoned the last meager vestiges of their humanness to all that concrete, glass, steel, and technology.

While Officer Saner leafed through one more motorcycle magazine, did one more word find, before he flipped the intercom switch to listen to one more goddamn complaint—a complaint he had no intention of doing anything about.

Chapter Eighteen

Safety and Security

Nurse, nurse, help, I can't breathe. Please, I can't breathe."

I could just see down the hall of the SHU six burly men dressed in black with helmets on their heads, the plastic visors pulled down, carrying an inmate in, his arms and legs stretched out like a bug on a display board.

But this bug wasn't dead or anesthetized. Instead he stiffened his legs and jerked his arms, and stiffened his arms and jerked his legs.

"Help, nurse, I can't breathe," he shouted, then moaned. "Oh, please somebody help me."

"Your cooperation is requested. Once you are secured in the cell you will be examined by medical personnel," I heard the ERT officer at the front of the group recite in a clipped, controlled voice.

A CO carrying a handheld video camera and a nurse in a bright balloon-covered smock walked behind them.

I recognized the nurse. She was the one who'd tickled Warden Root so much with her question about the intercom button when he'd given us our tour of the SHU a little over a year ago.

"Help, I can't breathe, I'm choking," the inmate's voice erupted from the center of those tangled limbs.

"Your cooperation is requested," the commander barked back.

Those prescribed words seemed to be the only thing keeping his rage and frustration in check.

That strange procession moved quickly out of sight, but the man's pleas and the officers' responses echoed down the metal and stone hallway to where I was sitting.

Then I heard a distant steel and glass cell door rattle open and clank shut.

Even behind that door I could still make out the inmate's muffled sobs and the CO's shouted commands to strip down, to get into the shower. Now!

I shifted in my chair, turning away from that end of the hallway.

I looked up from what I had been pretending to read and met Dario's black eyes. I was surprised to see that they were wide with fear. They studied me through the thick safety-glass window that separated us.

Dario was back in jail; and somehow he had managed to become a senior in high school even after his years of living on the streets or in jail. He was bright, quick, funny, and articulate, all of which might explain how he had made it this far in an educational system that seemed more set up to obstruct kids like him—poor, minority, and disenfranchised—than help them succeed.

But his obvious talents didn't explain why he was sitting in the SHU, and not for the first time.

"Dario, how'd you get yourself thrown in here again?" I asked when I went there to bring him schoolwork. "I thought you were determined to stay out of trouble so you could finish up this diploma."

In order for us to talk, we had to speak through the waist-high food tray slot.

That was easy for Dario. Despite his over six-foot frame, he could fold up on his cell's concrete floor and lean against his concrete bed. I had to squat outside in the hallway with my feet falling asleep.

If we didn't want our conversation broadcast to the rest of the block, we had to switch mouth and ear back and forth to the opening.

"I couldn't let that jerk talk to my man that way," he said, as though his answer was logical enough that it was a waste of his time to explain further.

"You know Karlos? Short dude from P.R.? His English isn't so good and that asshole CO, MacCameron, was giving him a hard time about going to the law library," he shouted loud enough for everybody to hear. This was one escapade he didn't mind having an audience for, especially Saner, the CO in charge.

"Karlos was getting all frustrated because he couldn't understand, so I figured I'd help out. But instead of thanking me, CO told me to mind my fuckin' business. That's exactly what he said, 'Mind your fuckin' business.' So I spit on him.

"And I spit on that fat-assed, old, white bitch, Sergeant Borders, screaming that she'd have me locked up in the SHU for the rest of my bid. Yeah, right!"

"Well, you may be smart," I growled back, annoyed to see one of my brightest students in this place, "but you sure are stupid."

Dario stared down at his hands in his lap.

"What can I tell ya, Mr. C? I'm bad," he answered, leaning in closer to the slot and lowering his voice. It wouldn't do for the gov'ment to hear him fessing up.

That morning though, when the ERT brought the inmate in, I wasn't there to hear his confession or to yell at him. I was there to give Dario his state-mandated English exam. If he passed this test, he would earn his high school diploma, the first one in his family, he'd told me.

It was a long and grueling exam with hours of reading and responsive writing.

But that was okay with Dario.

"I got lots of time on my hands." He shrugged when I made apologetic noises about the test.

"Besides, you know me, I love to read, and, well, writing's okay, I guess."

For me, though, it meant hours of sitting in that long, drafty hallway, in full view of everybody—Saner at the control desk, the other inmates in the other cells, and the cameras perched in every available corner.

I had a lot to keep me busy. I brought papers to be corrected and my grade book to be updated. I moved the plastic chair Saner reluctantly gave me into the best light and arranged everything around me.

Dario set himself up on the bed. He leaned against the concrete wall, using his lap as a desk.

Once I gave Dario his instructions, we both settled into what we had to do. Even though the state ed department notoriously chose literature texts that were dull and obscure, I was happy to see that Dario was soon lost to the outside world.

Until the ERT came bursting into the SHU.

If you watched Dario move around the county jail when he wasn't on lockdown you'd think, "Here's a kid who's not afraid of anything."

His size gave that impression. Although he was tall, there was nothing lank about him. In his teens he had acquired the muscled heft of a twenty-five-year-old, a heft that, unlike the other guys on the block, he didn't have to work very hard at.

But even with that brawn, he never bullied. He was too smart for that.

Instead he used what he had. His coal-black complexion, his broad face and round, deep-set eyes, his firm tight jawline—he worked it all for whatever effect he was after. Charm or threat, correctional staff or inmate, he always got what he wanted. Until that is, he was bad.

That's why I was startled that morning when I looked up and saw him staring at me, his eyes filled with an animal terror, his lips slightly parted as though he was panting, and all his papers fallen on the floor.

If there hadn't been that thick glass between us, I would've reached over and reassured him that everything was okay. I would've promised him that I wouldn't let anything happen to him, the way I would've promised a little boy still tangled up in the tatters of a bad dream.

But I knew that there wasn't any comfort I could give or protection I could guarantee this nineteen-year-old boy trapped in the nether world of jail.

Unlike Dario I'd never been ensnared in the real-life nightmare of six super-dieseled men, dressed in black, with black combat boots and black, padded, chest protectors, their faces hidden behind reflective visors, one arm holding up a Plexiglas shield, running into my room, screaming at me, demanding that I drop to the floor, facedown.

I'd never been walking down the hallway back from the visiting room, feeling happy and sad and lonely from seeing my girl, or my mother, or my baby boy who'd finally learned to say "Papa," who'd actually said it while he was sitting on my lap, when a rank of those same phantoms on their way to haunt some other inmate's dreams thundered past me, their angry black boots slapping the floor, shouting at me to kneel down, face the wall, put my hands behind my head. I'd never had my head shoved against the wall by the last CO in that line because he thought I looked around too soon.

"I'll be right back, Mr. C," Dario said, breaking the stare and bending close to the opening so only I could hear. "I gotta pee."

He stood up.

As he slipped into the bathroom cubicle no bigger than a shower stall, he looked over my shoulder. Then, like magic, his fear vanished.

"Excuse me, sir."

I hadn't heard Saner coming up behind me, but it explained the sudden disappearance of Dario's fear. He couldn't let the enemy see the terror in his eyes.

"I don't want to disturb you and the young man taking his test," Saner politely smirked, bending slightly at the waist toward me.

"I just want to assure you that the gentleman you saw being escorted in is perfectly safe. The emergency response team was forced to administer pepper spray due to his uncooperative and assaultive behavior."

He sounded like he was reading off some handout on communication skills from one of the refresher courses the COs all grumbled about taking at the training academy.

"Once he took a shower, which he was reluctant to do, the effects of the spray were washed away."

There wasn't much for me to say except, "Thanks, officer," as though this cardboard cutout of a butler had brought me the mail on a silver salver.

Somehow, though, I was the one who ended up feeling embarrassed and humiliated.

Nevertheless, I understood what was behind this exaggerated politeness.

I was a civilian, and a civilian should never have witnessed what had just happened.

My suspicion was confirmed when I saw Captain Inez, the captain in charge of the SHU, glaring down the hall at us. He stood behind the control desk, his starched white shirt rolling over his barrel chest, listening in like a newspaper drama critic preparing his review.

Saner turned around from me and shrugged at the captain. He shoved his hands into his pockets and sauntered back toward the control desk.

Captain Inez nodded his satisfaction, then without waiting for Saner to make it back, turned and left.

Dario didn't come out of the bathroom until after the ERT left, and the captain left, and Saner settled behind his motorcycle magazine, and the newest inmate's moans trailed off into whimpers.

He didn't look at me. He picked up his papers from the floor, settled against the wall, and looked for where he left off.

Slowly the SHU settled back into its earlier silence.

I knew it didn't have to be that way.

After an incident like this morning's, it could have become an echo chamber of curses and screams. One man's desperate calls for help could have ricocheted back as rage and hatred, as the other men emptied their lungs over their own violations and the violations of all the other men who'd been locked up for all those decades before them.

I'd seen it happen before in the rest of the jail.

An inmate was pulled out of the hallway and made to stand spread-eagled against the wall, roughly patted down, then cuffed and taken down to the booking department. Or the same squad of faceless men stormed a block and took some inmate down or trashed an entire dorm, flipping mattresses, dumping out lockers, throwing away books and food and family pictures.

After incidents like that the place could explode. Arguments escalate, fights break out, and chaos threatens.

Then suddenly the PA system would squawk a code, and hallway COs would shout and herd inmates back to their blocks. They would empty the classrooms, the clinics, the chapel, the visiting rooms. The whole place would be on security lockdown.

But that wasn't what happened that morning.

Instead, the men in the SHU were silent, the place, calm.

Even though the unit was deliberately designed to keep the inmates cut off from each other, the men were deeply connected in ways none of us outside those cells could ever understand.

That morning they all knew it was a big day for one of their own, and so I wasn't surprised when I walked down the hall toward Dario's cell that several guys called out to me to wish him luck.

One old guy, he had to be close to seventy, balding, his face creased and battered as an old brown boot, waved his arms to get my attention. He motioned me over to his tray slot.

"That's a good boy in there, Teach," he said, his voice graveled with years of smokes and booze. "Smart, too. You tell him I'm gonna keep these guys real quiet for him sos he can think."

I thanked him and told him I'd pass on his words of encouragement, all the while wondering what an old-timer like that could've done to get himself thrown into the SHU.

Dario gave me a big smile when I delivered the message.

"That's Old Cal, he's kinda crazy. He likes the boys"—Dario smiled and shrugged—"but he's okay."

Then he settled down on his bed ready to do justice to Old Cal's expectations.

That morning the SHU was peaceful, almost rapt with concentration and good wishes.

Until those six black clad, burly men, helmets on their heads, plastic visors pulled down, carried an inmate in, his pleas for air and help shattering the silence.

I didn't get much done that afternoon. I kept hearing that stomp of boots, those strangled cries for help, that clipped voice barking out commands.

Instead I sat in the cold, dim hallway and shuffled papers and watched Dario's cell fill up with sunlight.

Not Dario. He accomplished quite a lot.

Somehow, in that muddle of tension and confusion, he managed to finish his test and, with the quick perusal I was able to give it, did very well.

As I walked down the hallway toward Saner, slouched in his swivel chair behind the control desk staring at me, I saw Old Cal.

He was standing, waiting for news. His solemn and worried face was pressed against the glass so that he could see me as I came by.

When I was level with his cell he slowly raised his hand in a quizzical "thumbs-up."

I gave him a big nod.

"Thanks, Teach, thanks for getting the boy through," he shouted out to me.

"No, Cal," I mouthed back to him. "No. Thank *you*. It was you and the other guys who kept things quiet and under control."

Those men, the worst of the bunch, the biggest troublemakers, the most violent and dangerous, had done something that neither DOC nor I in all my many years at the county lockup had been able to do. They'd kept the usual welter of jail life at bay. They gave

Dario real safety and security by holding out to him the promise of a different kind of life. It was a promise that said, "Come on, kid, do a good job, because your life don't have to be the way it's been for us."

"No, Cal, you were as good as your word," I called as I turned away toward Saner and the front door. "Dario could'nt've done it without you!"

And the old man's worn and lined face grew younger by years with a big, gleeful smile.

Afterword

I couldn't fuckin' believe it. My girl just gave me that bomber jacket for my birthday," Tony, a nineteen-year-old Italian from the Bronx, complained, lamented really.

"I mean, like, man, I was just workin' on soften' it up, wearing it everywhere.

"And my Yankee cap? Christ, man, I loved that cap. Gone. Dead."

It was at the end of class, one of those afternoons when I taught on the block. The sun had long gone to the other side of the building. The few tables we used as desks were still nested together in the center of all the usual chaos—toilets flushing, TVs blaring, an argument ready to bust out on the tier, the CO's shouts to "cut the shit."

That day a few of the guys had stayed around to talk. They weren't ready to leave, to break the illusion that they were somewhere else.

Instead, they pushed back their chairs and stretched their legs out in front of them. They crossed their arms over their chests, for once not in that "fuck you" posture they so often fended the world off with, but like old men tired, relaxed after a hard day at work. They talked about their "property," the things—shirts, jeans, ball caps, sneakers—that DOC took from them when they came into booking and that were locked away for safekeeping while they served their time.

"Dead?" I asked, collecting the few pencils the guys hadn't succeeded in swiping. I never *could* let a remark like that pass.

"Yeah, man—ah, sorry, Teach—dead. Gone. Over. There's no way I'm wearing any of that shit when I get bounced.

"I don't want the smell of this place on me. I don't want nothing about this place followin' me. Besides, those clothes are bad luck."

Tony said it as though it was the leather jacket's fault he got arrested and not the loaded gun and the stash of coke he carried in the jacket's pockets.

"As soon as I get outta here? I'm burning it all," he explained, and the other guys nodded sagely.

I'd heard that same conversation any number of times during my years in the jail.

It didn't matter how long a kid was locked up for—a few weeks, a few months, back-to-back bullets—they all talked about their property the way young professionals out in the world talked about their investment portfolios.

Property was what defined who they were. Brand names, style, color, cost, weight in gold, all were slapped down on the table like playing cards trumping each other's bid.

Nobody won that game, though, because whatever their boast, they still sat in the same hot, dirty, paint-chipped dayroom, wearing the same county-issued orange scrubs and the same county-issued slip-on blue canvas sneakers.

Nobody won because when they got out of lockup, each of them would throw their property away, burn it, bury it, sell it if they could find a sucker, they didn't care who inherited their bad luck just as long as it didn't bounce back on them.

Everyone had their day, though, that day when the CO hung up the security phone and yelled, so the whole block could hear, "Sandleman or Rodriguez or Franklin, on the discharge."

Then, before the escort hustled the soon-to-be-free man down to booking for processing, he'd have his round of backslaps and half hugs, of shout-outs, of "Yo, man, one love," "Peace," "Stay out this time." Backing toward the door, weaving and bobbing like a triumphant boxer leaving the ring, he'd follow the CO out and disappear into the world—at least for a while.

Once he was finished in booking, signing what had to be signed, the CO handed him a black plastic bag with his property in it.

It didn't matter if a guy got arrested in August and left in February. What he came in with is what he left in—baggy nylon shorts, oversize tee, flip-flops.

There might be six inches of snow on the ground. There might be an icy wind howling across those old abandoned farm fields. Didn't matter. There was no way he was going to take the warm clothes DOC offered him from the Salvation Army stash.

The first time I saw some big, goofy, smiling kid flip-flopping down the shoveled walkway to the bus stop, black plastic sack flung over his shoulder like a jailhouse parody of Santa, I thought it was a matter of fashion.

But listening to the guys talk, I soon realized there was more to it than that. No way was this young brother going to step off the 15 bus after being locked up for six months and let his buddies—the same guys hanging out on the same corner in front of the same bodega, whatever the weather—see him in used church clothes, "indigent clothes," the guys cursed them. They treated the handouts DOC offered as though they were the ankle bracelets judges slapped on some of them as part of their release, set to snag them back in again the first time they even *thought* about breaking probation.

But they didn't just want to destroy their property. They wanted to banish jail from memory altogether. They insisted, demanded, begged me to get rid of all their school papers when they were discharged.

"Yo, Mr. C, no offense, but what am I gonna do with that stuff back in my crib?" they'd ask when I handed them their folder of schoolwork to take home.

To me, that manila folder—battered, torn, doodled, and smudged, thick with accomplishment—was something to be proud of.

Not to them. They saw it as one more piece of state's evidence turned against them, proof that they fucked up, that po-lice won, that the system got them one more time.

Never again.

"I don't want that. But you're not going to *keep* it, are you?" they'd panic. "It's got my name on it! Man, I don't want nothing in here with my name on it. Throw it away."

Jail had its own siren call, and it was their name.

So the day before they were scheduled to leave, Kahlil, Jonathan, Wade, Luis, Reynaldo, whoever was waiting to hear that magic incantation "on the discharge," would sit hunched over the classroom wastebasket and shred paper after paper, anything with their name, their writing, even their prints on it.

A lot got lost in that silent, systematic purge: job or school references staff had written; copies of hard-won GEDs; important phone numbers; lists of appointments and who to see for social services, school, jobs, treatment.

Determined to destroy prison's secret power over them, they were willing to sacrifice everything.

But as anyone who's been inside knows, you never leave jail, and jail never leaves you.

These young guys might take home beefed-up bodies and the merit badge of doing time—useful credentials in the hood—but they still leave with the empty purse of months, sometimes years, spent in adult lockup. And they leave with the anguish, resentments, and hostilities of what they saw in jail, of what they had done to them, and of what they did; anguish, resentments, and hostilities as deep and livid as the bullet and knife wounds they barely survived; forces that will pull them back to the streets, back to the reckless life that will inevitably pull them back to prison more than any court-mandated ankle bracelet.

It wasn't much different for the COs, the men and women who spend their own long bids behind bars. At the end of their shift, Ms. Wharton, Ramos, O'Shay, Saner might escape in their expensive cars and SUVs, ransom for long hours of overtime. But no matter how smooth or luxurious the ride home is they nevertheless land right back where they started, back with the same troubled families, the same fractured marriages, the same loneliness and stress, the same health problems. They land right back in the same angry stupor of booze, drugs, tobacco, gambling, even God, anything to blunt the onus of keeper and kept, to blunt the dread of the next day's alarm clock.

And me? Although I have my credentials as a jailhouse teacher, I certainly don't have the beefed-up body or the expensive car. I don't have the property to burn, and I don't believe that destroying it would free me of everything I'd experienced every day there. Yet, just like the kids I taught and the men and women I worked with, I carry the memories and dreams and, at times, the tight-fisted nightmares of jail.

And like my students, I have my own manila folder—battered, torn, doodled, and smudged, thick with accomplishment. It's filled with the things that have meant the most to me, things that I would never dream of destroying: a poem from Kahlil, a copy of the letter Warren never sent to Claude Brown, a drawing that Pyro did just before he was deported, along with the notes and poems of thanks other locked-away kids have written me over the years.

I even have Ms. Wharton's postcard, its white-stone hotel, blue sky, and sandy beach dazzled by the Bahamian sun. Rereading the hurried, scrawled message, I still find her *Ha-ha* as baffling as it was the day Sergeant Portal handed the postcard to me. Until, that is, I remember the most important lesson I learned during my ten years in county lockup, a lesson as deep and livid as the wounds many of my students carried away with them, as enduring as the stresses the COs shoulder, that we are all children of disappointment.

Acknowledgments

Many thanks to my agent, Jon Sternfeld, who from the first, championed the book and worked tirelessly to find it a home in the broader world.

I am grateful to all the people at Beacon Press who, once they read the stories of these locked-up young people, were determined that their voices be heard. I especially thank my editor, Amy Caldwell, for her sensitivity to the world these kids lived in and the language needed to describe it, and for her warm and respectful approach to the writing—and the writer. Thanks also to Alex Kapitan, editorial assistant, who was always helpful and treated me with a welcoming courtesy that made me feel like a special houseguest.

My years in education have taught me that teachers come in many guises. I learned much from correctional officers John Houston and Gerry Washington who in a single day brought more humanity into jail than many others managed to do in years, and from Fabiola Piperis, whose many efforts, despite institutional inertia, helped young offenders break the cycle of failure.

To my colleagues in incarcerated education, I owe many thanks, especially to Maria Morgan and Donnie Simmons for their commitment and ongoing work with the Incarcerated Youth Program.

I am deeply grateful to Joan Edwards-Acuña and Kay Schonberg for their dedication to society's throwaways and for their friendship and confidence in the project. Faithful readers, they kept me going.

I want to thank Aliza (Zizi) Ansell, a staunch advocate for people at-risk, who worked mightily in all the ways she could think of to ensure that the stories of these locked-up kids got out there. Her enthusiasm for the book made her a one woman cheerleading squad. Thanks to Emily Fox, whose belief in my writing set me on her own trail of connections. I am grateful to Anne Fox, skilled writer, editor, and friend, who urged me, nudged me, pushed me, along the road toward publication with her knowledge, wisdom, and kindness.

And lastly, this book would never have been written if it wasn't for the sustaining love and efforts of family and longtime friends. My older brother Walt opened the world of literature to me when, after he realized that this little brother wasn't going away, he shared his own books and his love of words. His confidence in me as a writer and his persistent nagging—"I think you're ready"—helped this book see print. Many thanks to Amy Olver for her years of friendship and everyday wisdom, and her encouraging and funny late-night e-mails. To Kathleen Duffy-Silcott, friend of many decades, I owe more than thanks. Long before my words saw the light of day she insisted on calling me her "friend, the writer." Her insistence on that identity helped me hold fast to who I was and what I loved to do. And finally to Rick Hart, to whom I owe incalculable gratitude for his many years of support, generosity, and love.

To all these, and to the hundreds of young men and women who passed through my jailhouse classroom, I offer a deep bow of gratitude.